STEPHEN A. SWAILS

Southern Biography Series

STEPHEN A. SWAILS

BLACK FREEDOM FIGHTER

IN THE CIVIL WAR
AND RECONSTRUCTION

GORDON C. RHEA

LOUISIANA STATE UNIVERSITY PRESS

BATON ROUGE

Published with the assistance of the Michael H. and Ayan Rubin Fund

Published by Louisiana State University Press
lsupress.org

Manufactured in the United States of America
First printing

Designer: *Mandy McDonald Scallan*
Typeface: *Sentinel*
Printer and binder: *Sheridan Books, Inc.*

Frontispiece/jacket photograph of Stephen Atkins Swails is from the Massachusetts
MOLLUS Collection, U.S. Army Heritage and Education Center, Carlisle, Pa.

Library of Congress Cataloging-in-Publication Data
Names: Rhea, Gordon C., author.
Title: Stephen A. Swails : Black freedom fighter in the Civil War and
    Reconstruction / Gordon C. Rhea.
Other titles: Black freedom fighter in the Civil War and Reconstruction
Description: Baton Rouge : Louisiana State University Press, [2021] | Series: Southern
    biography series | Includes bibliographical references and index.
Identifiers: LCCN 2021010896 (print) | LCCN 2021010897 (ebook) | ISBN
    978-0-8071-7626-9 (cloth) | ISBN 978-0-8071-7656-6 (pdf) | ISBN 978-0-8071-7657-3 (epub)
Subjects: LCSH: Swails, Stephen A., 1832–1900. | Reconstruction (U.S. history, 1865–1877) |
    Southern States—Race relations. | South Carolina—Politics and government—1865–1950. |
    United States. Bureau of Refugees, Freedmen, and Abandoned Lands—Officials and
    employees—Biography. | African American legislators—South Carolina—Biography. | United
    States. Army. Massachusetts Infantry Regiment, 54th (1863–1865) | United States—History—
    Civil War, 1861–1865—Participation, African American. | African Americans—South
    Carolina—Biography. | South Carolina—Biography.
Classification: LCC F274.S93 R44 2021 (print) | LCC F274.S93 (ebook) |
    DDC 975.7/041092 [B]—dc23
LC record available at https://lccn.loc.gov/2021010896
LC ebook record available at https://lccn.loc.gov/2021010897

CONTENTS

ILLUSTRATIONS

Figures

Stephen Atkins Swails *frontispiece*

Maps

PREFACE

One fall day in 1978, brothers Jimmy and Edward Moore were driving through Kingstree, a small town in rural South Carolina. As they turned off Main Street onto North Brooks Street, between the Carolina Warehouse and Redmond Funeral Home, they spotted an antique trunk and a basket made from elm bark, apparently set beside the road for removal by one of the town's trash trucks. Later, their curiosity aroused, the brothers turned around and drove back for a closer look. The items were gone; a trash truck had already arrived and was carting them to the town's dump.

Later that day, Jimmy passed the trash dump on his way to a boat landing on the Black River. There he spied the trunk, standing upright and waiting for the county's bulldozer to crush it and cover it with dirt. He got out, walked over to the trunk, and opened it. Inside were reams of papers and documents dating from the Civil War and Reconstruction years. Curious to learn more, he heaved the trunk onto his truck and took it home. That evening he and his brother looked through the contents. Inside were Stephen Swails's army records, booklets and ledgers from the Freedmen's Bureau with the names of long-forgotten former slaves, telegraph messages, and letters, including an exchange between Swails and Governor Wade Hampton concerning an attempt on Swails's life.

Although the brothers had never heard of Stephen Swails, they recognized the documents' historic worth and presumed that the correspondence bearing Governor Hampton's signature might have some value. They hauled the materials to Samuel McIntosh of the county historical society, who gave them $75 as a "finder's fee" and then donated the contents to the South Caroliniana Library at the University of South Carolina.

Stephen Swails's home once stood where the Carolina Warehouse was later built, which helps explain why his papers ended up there. The last-second rescue of his personal papers was but the most recent astonishing event surrounding this remarkable man's life. Swails, it developed, was a long-forgotten central participant in Kingstree's political history, in the story of African Americans' participation in the Civil War, and in South Carolina's Reconstruction experience.

Born in 1832 in Pennsylvania to parents that the census recorded as "mulatto," Swails grew up a free Black in a state that had abolished slavery, but whose African American citizens still labored under oppressive social and legal handicaps. In 1863, he volunteered for the most prominent African American regiment raised in the North—the 54th Massachusetts—distinguished himself in battle, and became the first Black man commissioned as a line combat officer in the US military.* After the war, he remained in South Carolina, where he was elected speaker pro tempore of the state senate during Reconstruction. He was instrumental in drafting the state's postwar constitution guaranteeing equal rights to African Americans and played an important role in securing the passage of legislation benefiting the state's newly liberated Black citizenry. He raised a family in the small South Carolina town of Kingstree, where he was elected mayor multiple times, practiced law, and became Williamsburg County's political "boss." Swails remained active in state politics after the end of Reconstruction and the restoration of white rule in 1877 but was ultimately forced to leave South Carolina by the white power structure, which threatened to kill him if he remained. Despite numerous threats against his life, he returned to South Carolina regularly and labored to advance the cause of Black candidates. Swails died in 1900 and remained largely forgotten for the next century.

Biographies of Civil War generals and major political figures appear by the score, but biographies of the nearly 200,000 African Americans who fought in the war are exceedingly rare. Swails's story is truly astounding. He was born into a society that relegated persons of African descent to the lowest social and economic rung yet rose to the pinnacle of political power, governing a hostile populace that viewed his race with hatred and distain. His life is a stirring tale of a determined man who overcame seemingly insurmountable obstacles and hardships. And

---

*Several accounts describe the 54th Massachusetts as the first Black regiment raised in the North. In fact, the 1st Kansas Colored Volunteer Infantry was raised in August 1862, more than a year after Kansas had been admitted to the Union, and was mustered into the Federal army in January 1863. The 54th Massachusetts was the second, but certainly the most widely known, Black regiment raised in the North.

while many of his achievements went up in flames with the end of Reconstruction and the return of white supremacy, his legacy lives on in the accomplishments of those who followed in his footsteps. Swails was a dynamic figure in the post–Civil War effort to ensure equal opportunity and treatment under the law for all citizens, Black and white.

Heading the list of the many people who assisted me in this project are William "Billy" Jenkinson and Hugh MacDougall. A prominent Kingstree attorney, Billy Jenkinson became fascinated with Swails after learning of him in the 1990s and devoted his considerable energy to unearthing information about the man from a myriad of sources. He also delivered several talks about Swails, was instrumental in getting a historical marker installed at the site of Swails's home, and organized an event culminating in the placement of a granite memorial at Swails's gravesite. Several years ago he met my wife and, being familiar with my writing, asked her to arrange an introduction, which she did. Billy's enthusiasm for getting Swails's story before the public was contagious, and he has generously shared with me his ideas and the fruits of his historical research. This book is as much his as it is mine, and I am deeply grateful to him for his partnership in this endeavor and his determination to bring this story to life.

Hugh MacDougall, a former attorney and diplomat, devoted his retirement years to delving into the history of Cooperstown, New York. From that, he developed a special interest in Swails, who had lived in Cooperstown as a young man, and delivered presentations about him and drafted an unpublished article entitled "The Search for Stephen Swails," which contains a wealth of information about the former warrior and politician. Together, Jenkinson and MacDougall provided a sturdy foundation for my endeavor.

Unpublished manuscripts form the core of this book. Swails's personal papers contain a wealth of documents, letters, and the like, including correspondence with Governor Hampton about an attempt on his life by some of Hampton's supporters. Important in reconstructing Swails's immediate postwar years are the extensive Freedmen's Bureau records in the National Archives and his own letters to various governors during the Reconstruction years in the collections of the South Carolina Department of Archives and History (SCDAH), which help bring to life his tenure in the Freedmen's Bureau and in the South Carolina Senate.

I am especially grateful to Eric Emerson and Wade Dorsey of SCDAH for assisting me in locating relevant material in their extensive repository. Also helpful was Fergus Bordewich, author of *Bound for Canaan: The Epic Story of the Underground Railroad, America's First Civil Rights Movement* (2005), who shared with me his knowledge about the Underground Railroad and introduced me to Randolph Harris, an expert on the Underground Railroad in Pennsylvania. I am also deeply indebted to several historians who read my manuscript and suggested improvements and additional sources, including A. Wilson Greene, Eric Wittenberg, Kevin Levin, Bryce Suderow, and Sharon MacDonald. I am especially grateful for the assistance of Stephen R. Wise, the foremost historian of South Carolina's Low Country, who saved me from several errors of interpretation and introduced me to invaluable unpublished resources.

George Skoch, who crafted the maps for several of my former books, applied his talents to the maps that appear here and help explain the battles in which Swails fought. I also thank Rand Dotson, LSU Press editor-in-chief, who supported this endeavor from the outset, and Kevin Brock, who once again applied his editorial skills to sharpen my prose. My sons Campbell and Carter read my manuscript and made important suggestions, and as always, my wife, Catherine, was a constant companion, inspiration, and editor in my quest to understand and document the life of this remarkable American.

STEPHEN A. SWAILS

CHAPTER ONE

An Angel of God Come Down to Lead the Host of Freedom

Stephen Atkins Swails was born in Columbia, Pennsylvania, on February 24, 1832. Census reports variously describe his father, Peter Swails, as Black or mulatto, originally from Maryland, and most likely a fugitive slave who, like so many others, had sought refuge in this free state. His mother, Joanna Atkins Swails, also hailed from Maryland. Some accounts refer to her as white, although US census records identify her as mulatto, which raises the possibility that she, too, had been enslaved.

The infant Swails entered the world in an epicenter for the divisive forces convulsing the nation: slavery, the abolitionist movement, and evolving race relations between whites and free Blacks. No one, however, anticipated the explosive events that occurred in Columbia in 1834, when Swails was two and a half years old. It was a warm Saturday evening in August, and the small Pennsylvania village nestled on the Susquehanna River seemed placid and calm. In Columbia's Black quarter, called Tow Hill, the Swailses and other African American families were finishing their dinners, while parents were tucking their children into bed. Race riots had shaken New York, Philadelphia, and other Northern metropolises this summer of 1834, but such violence seemed impossible in Columbia. After all, the town was a terminal on the Underground Railroad, along which many of the Black inhabitants had escaped from slavery. Columbia was predominantly white but boasted a large and relatively prosperous Black population, composing some 15 percent of its citizenry. In the minds of local African Americans, Columbia was a sanctuary from the horrors they had endured as slaves in the South. It was a land where they could enjoy the fruits of freedom.

Then came the heavy tramp of footsteps, the shattering of windows, and angry insults screamed into the night. A mob, primarily white teenagers from working-class families, rolled through Tow Hill, cursing the frightened Black families huddling low in their homes, threatening their lives and property. Every night for four nights, the terror continued, increasing in intensity. Many families fled to the hills above town, where they remained in hiding for several days while waiting for the violence to subside. The riots culminated on Tuesday night, when a mob of fifty whites, including some older members of the town's prestigious families, descended on Tow Hill. This time the intruders remained until 2:00 A.M., shouting racial epithets, throwing rocks through windows, and firing guns. Cringing in his home, trembling from fear, little Stephen Swails experienced it all.

The editor of the local newspaper, the Columbia Spy, decried the vandalism and terror but blamed the violence on the local Black residents' "own imprudence," spawned by their "foolish notions of equality until they had become unbearably insolent." The white and Black races, he concluded, "never can, never ought to be amalgamated," leading him to recommend that the Blacks return to Africa. "Must the poor honest citizens," he asked, referring, of course, to the town's white population, "fly from their native place that a band of disorderly negroes may revel with the money that ought to support the white man and his family?"

A meeting of the town's white working class, held a few days after the violence had subsided, underscored the riot's economic underpinning and condemned "the practice of others in employing the negroes to do that labor which was formerly done entirely by whites." The cause of "the late disgraceful riots throughout every part of the country may be traced to the efforts of those who would wish the poor whites to amalgamate with the blacks," the meeting's participants announced, expressing concern "that the poor whites may gradually sink into the degraded condition of the negroes—that, like them, they may be slaves and tools, and that the blacks are to witness their disgusting servility to their employers and their unbearable insolence to the working-class."

Several circumstances had made Columbia a popular destination for escaped slaves seeking refuge, including its sizeable free Black population, its location at a major Susquehanna River crossing, and the Columbia Abolition Society's assistance. As the 1820s progressed, the town became a major terminal of the Underground Railroad, the name given to a secretive network of hiding places for escaped slaves on the way from the slaveowning states to Canada and to other parts of the United States where Black fugitives could live without fear of recapture. According to local lore, the term "Underground Railroad" originated in Columbia and referred to the fact that fugitive slaves who made it that far seemed to disappear, leaving their pursuers to surmise that "there must be an underground railroad somewhere."

Columbia also afforded its Black residents an opportunity to earn a living wage. Several of them fared better than that, leading a modern scholar to refer to Columbia as "The Black Eldorado." One of the town's prominent Black entrepreneurs was Stephen Smith, president of a local bank and owner of a profitable lumber and real estate businesses with his partner, William Whipper. By 1833, Smith owned six houses, six lots, livestock, stocks, bonds, and a pleasure carriage. He and Whipper actively participated in the Underground Railroad by hiding runaways in the false end of a boxcar carrying their products to Philadelphia and on barges plying the Pennsylvania Canal to Pittsburgh.

Not all of Columbia's white residents, however, took kindly to their Black neighbors' success. Smith in particular aroused their ire, and working-class whites began to fear the newcomers as competitors for their jobs. Racial prejudice also figured conspicuously, culminating in the explosive outpouring of violence against Columbia's Black population in 1834. The four days of violence that August were only the beginning. On September 2, a mob drove one of Swails's neighbors from his home and tore down his porch and part of his house. The rioters then broke into Smith's office, ransacking it, scattering his papers in the street, and unsuccessfully attempting to topple the building. Another public meeting of Columbia's white workers passed resolutions encouraging Blacks to sell their homes and businesses, to stop harboring Black transients, to "devise some means to prevent the further influx of colored persons to this place," and to cooperate in returning fugitive slaves to their "rightful owners."

Concerned that the town was becoming too dangerous for Black businessmen, Smith ran a notice in the local newspaper offering his entire lumber stock "at a reduced price, as I am determined to close my business at Columbia." No one took him up on his offer. Rioting against the Black population erupted again in early October, when a mob broke into four houses, destroyed their contents, and severely beat and slashed one occupant, leaving him "lying in his own blood amidst the rubble that shortly before was his home." Upset, too, that Black children were receiving an education, the mob broke into a school for African Americans, trashed the interior, and took special pains to destroy the pupils' inkstands and paper. The night's destruction closed with the burning of a carpenter's shop, where flames "reflected from the walls of the neighboring houses in excessive brightness, while the sky was illuminated by the conflagration," according to a newspaper report. "The exciting cause of this exhibition of illegal tumult and devastation was the reported recent marriage of a black man to a white woman," the article declared, "which re-kindled the smoldering ashes of former popular madness and afforded an opportunity to evil-disposed individuals to [reenact] past occurrences of disorder and destruction."

Unable to sell his lumber holdings, Smith endured threats against him into the next year. In February 1835, he received a letter advising him that his presence in the community was "not agreeable and the less you appear in the assembly of whites the better it will be for your black hide, as there are a great many in this place that would think your absence from it a benefit, as you are considered an injury to the real value of property in Columbia." Lest Smith missed the point, the letter concluded: "You had better take the hint and save—MANY."*

Stephen Swails's sojourn in Columbia was relatively brief, and he never wrote about his time there, perhaps because he had been too young to fully comprehend the horror of the violence targeted against his race. His Columbia days, however, were harbingers of the brutal racial prejudices that he would face in the coming years.

Most likely motivated by concern over Columbia's escalating violence against Blacks, Peter Swails moved his family to the nearby town of Manheim, where the numerous Mennonite and Dunker residents tended to be peaceful and welcoming. The uproar in Columbia over mixed-race

---

*Smith remained in Columbia until 1842, when he moved to Philadelphia. He was ordained a minister in the African Methodist Episcopal Church and increased his fortune by investments in real estate and negotiable papers. He continued his efforts to improve the lot of African Americans. Smith died in Philadelphia in 1873.

marriages might also have influenced his decision, as Peter apparently appeared black, while his wife, Johanna, looked white. In addition, considerably fewer Blacks lived in Manheim and presented less of an irritant to the white population there, reducing the odds of racial strife. Young Stephen spent his childhood and teenage years in this town, where his siblings Jesse, George, Rachael, Catherine, and Henrietta were born. According to census records from 1850, eighteen-year-old Stephen was attending school in Manheim.

Around 1855, the Swails family moved to Elmira, New York, only a few miles across the Pennsylvania border. Why they selected Elmira is not clear, although the reason might have involved that town's substantial Black population, its important role in the Underground Railroad, and the availability of work on the local railway and canal. John W. Jones, a freed slave, was a well-known conductor on the Underground Railroad and reputedly assisted some eight hundred slaves escape to freedom. Operating from his home behind the First Baptist Church, he would hide Black fugitives in a baggage car on the daily train to Niagara Falls, where they could disembark within walking distance of Canada. Sympathetic railroad workers assisted Jones and never charged for his "freight."*

In 1860, Stephen Swails, now twenty-eight, moved to Cooperstown, New York, and secured a waiter's position at the Keys Hotel on Main Street. The next year, he established a close romantic relationship Sarah Thompson, a Black woman employed as a servant in a local white household. Whether they were actually married is not clear, but they started a family together and soon had two children. In 1862, the Keys Hotel burned in a fire that swept Cooperstown's business district, bringing Swails's tenure there to a close. His employment for the next year is uncertain, although he listed himself in later documents as having been a "boatman," probably on the local canal.

On April 8, 1863, Swails took a step that would dramatically change his life. The American Civil War was in full swing, and he reported to Readville, Massachusetts, for induction as a three-year volunteer into the 54th Massachusetts Regiment, the first such outfit composed of Black volunteers from the North.

*Stephen Swails's sister Rachael married Jones.

A mean-spirited exchange between two Cooperstown newspapers three years after the end of the Civil War affords two markedly different pictures of Swails's last years in New York. When the articles appeared, Swails had won honors in the military and prominence in South Carolina as a Republican politician. Cooperstown's Democratic newspaper, the *Freeman's Journal,* printed a letter in its September 25, 1868, edition from an anonymous "C.J.S." describing Swails as "one of those mean, cunning, drunken, thieving 'niggers'" who worked as "a helper in the kitchen of a saloon, but was discharged for habitual drunkenness and dishonesty." According to C.J.S., Swails married a Black girl from Cooperstown named Thompson, with whom he had a child, but then "abandoned his wife and child and went to Massachusetts ... and went to war." Swails, he alleged, "followed or hunted after a White young man in this place, while he was on one of his drunks, with a large knife, for the purpose of getting even with him for some real or imaginary insult."

The editor of Cooperstown's Republican newspaper, the *Otsego Republican and Democrat,* painted a very different picture, noting that C.J.S., who happened to be Cooperstown's former mayor, had earned notoriety for frequenting local bars and abandoning his own wife. The editor went on to deny that Swails was mean, cunning, drunken, or thieving and countered that he had not lost his job for drunkenness but rather left home to volunteer for the army; that he "abandoned his wife and child just as every married man did who went to war, and in no other way"; and that he had been promoted for meritorious conduct "because of his valor and intelligence." C.J.S., the editor concluded, would have shown himself to be a better man had he not tried "to drag [Swails] down to the low level of himself." An anonymous writer seconded the editor's remarks and described C.J.S. as "the veriest bloat and loafer in this village" who had "driven his wife out of doors at the point of a dining fork [and] made it his daily habit to beat and knock her down," in the process making "himself an object of loathing to everyone familiar with his story."

Further exchanges between the rival papers confirmed that the debate over Swails's character and past behavior deserved to be taken with a grain of salt. On October 16, the *Freeman's Journal* termed Swails a "carpetbagger" and asserted that the *Otsego Republican and Democrat's* editor knew "that a majority of the northern people are opposed to a system so dishonest and unfair." The editor then fired back that he hoped "the South may be ruled *eternally* by loyal carpet baggers and scalawags. If she be, there will be before her the brightest future imaginable, and if her governments revert to the old Rebel element, the clock of her progress is not only stopped but set back."

Swails's fate over the next three years was tightly bound with the 54th Massachusetts, an African American regiment conceived and promoted by the Bay State's governor, John Albion Andrew. The New Englander's teenage interest in abolitionism and in William Lloyd Garrison's antislavery writings ripened into a lifelong devotion to end slavery and bring justice to the nation's Black population. Admitted to the bar in 1849, Andrew actively participated in the state's growing antislavery movement and served on Boston's Vigilance Committee, assisting escaped slaves. After passage of the Fugitive Slave Act in 1850, which required citizens of all states, including those where slavery had been abolished, to apprehend and return escaped slaves to their masters, Andrew specialized in defending fugitives and their allies. He emerged as a prominent spokesman in Boston's antislavery community and voiced strong support for John Brown's 1859 raid on Harpers Ferry, announcing that he was not interested in "whether the enterprise of John Brown and his associates in Virginia was wise or foolish, right or wrong; I only know that, whether the enterprise was one or the other, John Brown himself was right."

Riding a wave of popularity, Andrew headed his state's delegation to the Republican National Convention in 1860 and was nominated as the party's candidate for governor. He won the election and was sworn in on January 2, 1861. He openly used his position to advance an antislavery agenda. Andrew also vocally supported enlisting and arming Black soldiers to fight in the war. When President Abraham Lincoln's Emancipation Proclamation went into effect on January 1, 1863, the governor secured permission from Secretary of War Edwin M. Stanton to raise "such corps of infantry for the volunteer military service as he may find convenient, such volunteers to be enlisted for three years or until sooner discharged, *and may include persons of African descent,* organized into separate corps." Andrew immediately threw himself into the project, whose "success or failure," he believed, would "go far to elevate or to depress the estimation in which the character of the Colored Americans will be held throughout the world."

To head the new regiment, Andrew wanted someone of impeccable reputation, hands-on military experience, and an abolitionist mindset. He selected Robert Gould Shaw, a captain in the 2nd Massachusetts Infantry and son of his longtime friend Francis George Shaw, a wealthy businessman devoted to the antislavery crusade. Robert was only twenty-five years old, but he filled the bill perfectly. "His bearing was graceful, as became a soldier and a gentleman," recalled an officer who later served under him. "His family connections were of the highest social standing, character, and influence."

Andrew asked Francis Shaw to forward a letter to Robert offering him command of the new Black regiment, observing that "the more ardent, faithful, and true Republicans would recognize in him a scion from a tree whose fruit and leaves have always contributed to the strength and healing of our generation." Shaw did as requested, but his son declined the offer and gave his father a letter to take back to the governor. Yet after more thought and consultation with his commanding officer, the younger Shaw changed his mind. "Please destroy my letter and telegraph to the governor that I accept," he requested of his father. Writing his fiancée, Annie Haggerty, he acknowledged that his decision might be "unpopular" with many, but that he was "convinced I shall never regret having taken this step, as far as I myself am concerned; for while I was undecided I felt ashamed of myself, as if I were cowardly."

Governor Andrew offered Norwood P. Hallowell, a captain in the 20th Massachusetts, the position of lieutenant colonel in the new regiment. Like Shaw, Hallowell came from a family that was strongly abolitionist in sentiment, and also like Shaw, he had seen active combat in several battles, including Antietam, where he and Shaw each had been wounded. Andrew considered him "a gallant and fine fellow, true as steel to the cause of humanity, as well as to the flag of the country."

Shaw and Hallowell returned to Boston and immersed themselves in the minutia of raising and organizing a regiment. Many Black leaders questioned the equity of an outfit composed of Black men but led by white officers. The prominent abolitionist Wendell Phillips addressed that issue head-on during a speech at Joy Street Baptist Church. Conceding that the arrangement smacked of unfairness, he pointed out the practical problems of persuading the general public to otherwise accept a regiment of Black troops. "If you cannot have a whole loaf, will you not take a slice?" he implored. "That is the great question for you to decide."

Advertisements appeared in Boston's newspapers under the heading, "TO COLORED MEN!" and announced, "Wanted—Good men for the 54th Regiment of Massachusetts Volunteers, of African Descent." Another broadside beseeched the city's "Colored Men to prove their Manhood and Loyalty by enlisting in the 54th Regiment," which would enable them to demonstrate that they were "not inferior in Courage and Patriotism to White Men." The renowned African American spokesman Frederick Douglass, himself an escaped slave who had long championed the idea of a Black regiment, embraced the new project. "When first the rebel cannon shattered the walls of Sumter, and drove away its starving garrison, I predicted that the war then and there inaugurated would not be fought out entirely by white men," he wrote in March 1863. "A war undertaken and brazenly carried on for the perpetual enslavement of colored men, calls logically and loudly for colored men to help suppress it." To Douglass, the way forward was clear. "Hence, with every reverse to the national arms, with every exultant shout of victory raised by the slaveholding rebels, I have implored the imperiled nation to unchain against her foes her powerful Black hand." Now the opportunity for Black people to fight for their own freedom had arrived, and Douglass devoted his full energy to promoting it. Two of his sons volunteered for service in the 54th Massachusetts.

When it appeared that the Bay State lacked sufficient Black men to fill the regiment, a committee formed to raise troops from neighboring states. Douglass took to the road, addressing enthusiastic audiences across the Northeast and reminding potential volunteers that Massachusetts was "first to break the chains of her slaves; first to make the Black man equal before the law; first to admit colored children to her common schools." He admonished the crowds that came to hear him speak to "go quickly and help fill up the first colored regiment from the North. The iron gate of our prison stands half-open. One gallant rush from the North will fling it wide open, while four millions of our brothers and sisters shall march out into liberty." Well-known abolitionists such as Garrison and Phillips added their voices in support, and volunteers began pouring into the 54th Massachusetts's camp at Readville, near Boston. According to one count, by the end of March, four of the new regiment's ten projected companies—each comprising one hundred soldiers—had been filled, and another one hundred volunteers arrived each week during April.

Shaw and Hallowell understood the importance of accepting only recruits of the highest caliber. "Public opinion in the North was either avowedly hostile to this scheme or entirely skeptical as to its value," Hallowell later wrote. The overall goal, Shaw told his fiancée, was to "prove that a Negro can be made a good soldier." Adding that he was aware of the "great prejudice" against a Black regiment, the young officer was certain that he "shan't be frightened out of it by its unpopularity; and I hope you will not care if it is made fun of." The recruits also recognized the seriousness of the undertaking. "Our people must know that if they are ever to attain to any position in the eyes of the civilized world, they must forego comfort, home, fear, and above all, superstition, and fight for it; make up their minds to become something more than hewers of wood and drawers of water all their lives," reported James H. Gooding, a Black correspondent for the *New Bedford Mercury* who joined the regiment. "Not a single volunteer," he observed, "does not appreciate the difficulties, the dangers, and maybe ignoble death that awaits him, if captured by the foe, and they will die in the field rather than be hanged like a dog; and when a thousand men are fighting for their very existence, who dare say them men won't fight determinedly? The greatest difficulty will be to stop them." Gooding heeded his own admonition. Later rising to the rank of corporal, he was captured in combat and died in the Confederate prisoner-of-war camp at Andersonville, Georgia.

To ensure that the soldiers were physically fit, each recruit was examined by a physician when he signed his enlistment papers, then examined again by the regiment's surgeon, Dr. Lincoln Stone, when he reported at Readville. According to Gooding, some 132 out of 500 applicants were rejected; Massachusetts's adjutant general put the rejection rate at a third of the men examined.

Captain Luis F. Emilio, who after the war penned the regiment's official history, noted that only a few of the volunteers had been slaves and that many were light skinned. Most of the recruits were literate, impressing one stranger who encountered several of them in a railway station with their ability to read and write and their decent appearance.

Conspicuous among the new soldiers was Stephen Swails, who fit Captain Emilio's recipe for the ideal Black soldier to a "T." He had been born free and was eloquent, literate, and so light skinned that people often presumed that he was white. According to his military records, Swails stood five feet, eight inches tall and had brown eyes, black hair, and a "light complexion." He impressed Shaw so much that the colonel quickly promoted him to first sergeant of Company F, retroactive to April 8, the day that he had arrived at camp.

Lieutenant Colonel Hallowell worked closely with Shaw to enforce a rigorous training program, one designed not only to prepare new inductees for the rigors of military service but also to imbue them with a sense of pride. Upon acceptance into service, Swails and the other new recruits were marched to a pond near the camp, disrobed, washed, and given a clean uniform to don while their old clothes were burned. The transformation, Hallowell wrote, was "quite wonderful." Preening in his new uniform, a recruit generally "straightened up, grew inches taller, lifted not shuffled, his feet, began at once to try, and to try hard, to take the position of the soldier."

Life at Readville was Spartan, but Swails and his companions adapted to it well. The barracks—one for each of the ten hundred-man companies—resembled huge wooden barns with bunks along each side. It rained a great deal that spring, compelling Swails and the others to train in mud. When the weather warmed, he and his company bathed in the pond. Shaw personally oversaw the rigorous training regimen. Reveille sounded at 5:30 in the morning, and drill began at 8:00, continuing for five hours. Long hikes and other strenuous endeavors filled the rest of the day, with lights out at 8:00 in the evening. By all accounts, morale was high. George Stephens, a Black correspondent for the *Weekly Anglo-African* and a soldier in the 54th, wrote that he did "not exaggerate when I say that there is no regiment superior, if equal to this in physique and aptitude of its men." A reporter from the *Springfield Republican* who attended a rally for the 54th noted that the Black soldiers displayed "rather an uncommon amount of muscle," but most importantly, "they marched well, they wheeled well, they stood well, they handled their guns well, and there was about their whole array an air of completeness, and order, and *morale*, such as I have not seen surpassed in any white regiment."

By May 13, with all ten companies filled, recruitment for the 54th closed. So many quality applicants remained, however, that Governor Andrew decided to raise yet another Black regiment, the 55th Massachusetts. On May 30, Hallowell was elevated to colonel and assigned to command the 55th. Taking his place as second in command of the 54th was his older brother, Major Edward Needles Hallowell, soon promoted to lieutenant colonel, whom one of Andrew's confidants described as "a tip top man, a regular Negrophile." Handsome and with a drooping mustache, he was no stranger to combat, having fought in the Peninsula Campaign, Antietam, and Fredericksburg as a lieutenant in the 20th Massachusetts.

On May 18, 1863, War Secretary Stanton directed Governor Andrew to send the 54th Massachusetts as soon as possible to South Carolina, where Union forces were raiding along the coast and attempting to capture Charleston. Shaw prepared to dispatch the regiment as soon as a transport ship arrived from New York.

At 6:30 on the morning of May 28, Sergeant Swails bid goodbye to the Readville camp, marched with his regiment to the local railroad station, and rode a train to Boston. Greeted with cheers by a large crowd, the soldiers marched several blocks to the statehouse, preceded by a band. Spectators crammed the sidewalks, windows, and balconies along the route, cheering and waving flags and handkerchiefs. Garrison, his hand resting on a bust of John Brown, greeted the soldiers from a balcony of Phillips's house. Farther along, Governor Andrew, along with Boston's mayor and a host of other notables, joined the procession. Swails and his compatriots paused for an hour in Boston Common, where Andrew addressed them from a reviewing stand and Shaw granted them a final opportunity to bid farewell to their families and friends. Then they reformed and continued to the wharf, their band playing "John Brown's Body." A local journalist reported, "Vast crowds lined the streets where the regiment was to pass, and the Common was crowded with an immense number of people such as only the Fourth of July or some rare event causes to assemble." In his opinion, "No white regiment from Massachusetts has surpassed the Fifty-fourth in excellence of drill, while in general discipline, dignity, and military bearing the regiment is acknowledged by every candid mind to be all that can be desired." The poet John Greenleaf Whittier later remarked that he could "never forget the scene as Colonel Shaw rode at the head of his men. The very flower of grace and chivalry, he seemed to me beautiful and awful, as an angel of God come down to lead the host of freedom to victory."

Not everyone, however, expressed delight at seeing a regiment of armed Black soldiers. As Shaw's men marched past the elite Somerset Club, some members drew the curtains closed while others hissed. "No scouts need ever to be sent out to discover such warriors, [because] twenty thousand negroes on the march would be smelled ten miles distant," predicted the *Boston Pilot,* a newspaper that reflected the hostile views of many in Boston's Irish community who feared that Blacks posed unwanted competition for their jobs, just as the white workers in Columbia had felt almost thirty years earlier. But while occasional groans could be heard as the 54th tramped past, the reception overall was enthusiastic and positive.

At one o'clock that afternoon, Swails and the rest of the regiment boarded the steamer *DeMolay,* which pushed off from the wharf and began their journey south. While officers luxuriated in staterooms, soldiers crowded between decks and slept on bunks. The next morning, Swails watched as they steamed past Martha's Vineyard and Nantucket; by morning on June 1, they were running down the North Carolina coast, accompanied by porpoises and sharks. He was treated to a brilliant sunset that evening—"the sun sank into the sea, red and fiery, gilding the horizon," one of his fellow voyagers recalled—but the next day a squall hit, replete with thunder and lightning, driving everyone below deck. The following day—June 3—the sun peeked through broken clouds, giving the seasick men of the 54th their first sighting of the South Carolina coast.

Little did Sergeant Swails and his companions imagine that they would soon become major participants in one of the war's most brutal bloodbaths.

CHAPTER TWO

One Plane of Ashes and Blackened Chimneys

At ten in the morning on June 3, 1863, the *DeMolay* motored past the Union fleet blockading Charleston's harbor, treating Swails and his companions to views of Fort Sumter and nearby Union ironclads. Three hours later, the transport arrived at Hilton Head, where a pilot drew alongside in a rowboat and guided the vessel to nearby Port Royal. Occupied by Union forces early in the war, the once-peaceful harbor now bustled with activity, serving as a hub for Federal military expeditions along the coast. Swails marveled at the sight of Port Royal Sound packed with warships, transports, and all manner of vessels. From the deck, he could see the small town swarming with soldiers and entrepreneurs catering to the glut of new arrivals exploring shops along Robber's Row, the main commercial street.

Soon after arriving in South Carolina, Colonel Shaw reported to Major General David Hunter, who directed him to take his regiment to the nearby town of Beaufort. Writing Governor Andrew about the 54th's safe arrival, Hunter assured him that "from the appearance of the men I doubt not this command will yet win a reputation and place in history deserving the patronage you have given them." He also requested the governor send him the other "colored regiment" that he understood Andrew was raising and promised that the additional outfit, along with the 54th, would be "profitably and honorably employed."

Setting off again, the *DeMolay* reached Beaufort the night of June 4, and at 5:00 the next morning, Swails and the 54th disembarked and marched through town. The sergeant looked on with pride at the turnout of soldiers and citizens lining the streets, all eager to see the first Black regiment composed of soldiers from the North. "Our reception was almost as enthusiastic here in Beaufort, as our departure from Boston was," one of Swails's companions wrote. "The contrabands did not believe we were coming," he added, but "they think now the kingdom is coming sure enough."

The regiment bivouacked in a cotton field on the Thompson plantation, about a quarter mile outside of town. Swails and the rest of the new arrivals erected shelters of bushes and blankets to fend off the blazing sun and battled swarms of insects. Colonel Shaw wrote home that it was "impossible to keep clean here for two hours—the fine sand covers everything."

Swails soon learned that he and his companions had sailed into a theater of war embroiled in controversy over the role of African American soldiers. A little over two years earlier—on April 19, 1861, only days after Fort Sumter surrendered to the Confederacy—President Lincoln had imposed a blockade along the rebellious states' coastline. The terrain from Charleston south presented a labyrinth of scrubby mosquito-infested islands, narrow winding waterways, and broad, virtually impenetrable marshes. This beautiful but inhospitable terrain was also home to plantations that relied on massive slave populations to cultivate lucrative crops of rice and Sea Island cotton.

In November 1861, a Union army-navy expeditionary force captured Port Royal Sound, the deepest natural harbor south of New York. Soon the Federals occupied the neighboring Sea Islands and the town of Beaufort. From Port Royal, the navy established a blockade of the South Carolina, Georgia, and East Florida coast. The army, headquartered on Hilton Head Island, protected the naval station and began developing plans for operations against nearby Confederate ports. Their objective was to gain footholds in strategic harbors along the Southern coast and ultimately occupy Savannah and Charleston, the two main port cities.

In March 1862, the War Department created from the expeditionary force the Department of the South, consisting of the troops stationed along the coasts of South Carolina, Georgia, and Florida, and placed it under the command of Major General Hunter, who was to cooperate with Commodore Samuel Francis Du Pont, leading the department's naval component, to capture Fort Pulaski on the Savannah River and "beat the enemy whenever and wherever an opportunity offers."

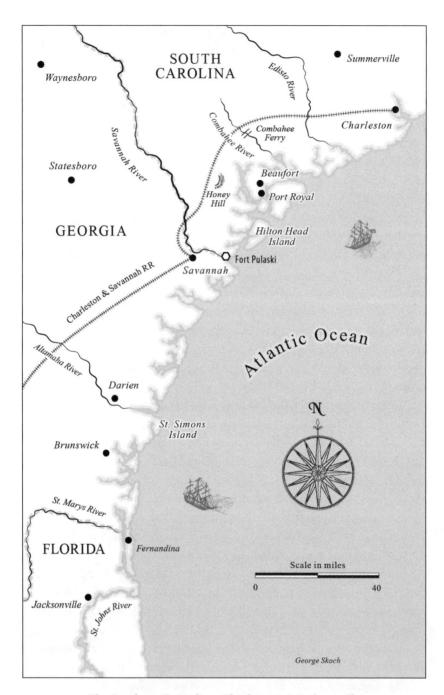

The Southern Coast from Charleston to Jacksonville

Hunter was a fervent abolitionist who boasted important political connections, including a friendship with President Lincoln. A contemporary remarked that he had "keen gray eyes, a long nose, slightly aquiline, a large mouth with corners slightly depressed and the whole shut with a sharp decisiveness." The general held strong views about how the war should be conducted and was not shy about expressing them. "It is time slavery had its quietus, we have been trifling long enough," he wrote early in the conflict, promising that if given the opportunity, he would "advance south, proclaiming the negro free and arming him as I go. The great God of the Universe has determined that this is the only way in which this war is to be ended, and the sooner it is done the better."

Hunter brought his abolitionist's zeal to his new assignment. Shortly after assuming his new duties, he requested from Secretary of War Stanton "authority to arm such loyal men as I can find in the country," implicitly referring to the large population of former slaves liberated by the Union occupation of the coastal territories. In order to better "know and distinguish these men at once," he also asked for 50,000 pairs of scarlet pantaloons. When a subordinate general promptly captured Fort Pulaski, Hunter on April 13 freed the slaves on Cockspur Island, where the fort was located. He then threw his energy into raising a regiment of former slaves liberated by Union incursions into the coast and the adjacent string of barrier islands, on May 8 declaring all slaves in South Carolina, Florida, and Georgia "forever free." Hunter expected the newly freed slaves to volunteer en masse, but not enough did, leading him to take the drastic step of ordering his district commanders "to send immediately to these headquarters, under a guard, all able-bodied negroes capable of bearing arms" to serve in the Union army. While many freedmen complied without protest, others resisted and were forcibly arrested and marched to Hunter's center at Hilton Head. Once there, the new soldiers donned red pants, blue coats, and broad-brimmed hats. Hunter's heavy-handed tactics offended much of the Black population, which viewed his corralling of its males as presaging another descent into servitude. A Federal agent working with the freedmen remarked that "never, in my judgment, did [a] major-general fall into a sadder blunder and rarely has humanity been outraged by an act of more unfeeling barbarity."

In his haste to free and arm former slaves, Hunter committed the cardinal sin of neglecting to secure Lincoln's approval. The president, concerned about alienating border states where slavery was still permitted, announced that "neither General Hunter, nor any other commander, nor person, has been authorized by the Government of the United States, to make proclamations declaring the slaves of any state free." The general's "supposed proclamation," he wrote, was "altogether void." Lincoln's rescission of Hunter's action also terminated the general's directive that freedmen be brought to Hilton Head and inducted into a newly formed regiment. Halting this harsh policy was, in the view of one observer, a salutary development. "This conscription, together with the manner of its execution," he noted, "has created a suspicion that the Government has not the interest in the negroes that it has professed, and many of them sighed yesterday for the 'old fetters' as being better than the new liberty."

Although Hunter's drive to secure approval for an armed African American regiment received some support in Congress, Lincoln continued to oppose the idea. "The President argued that the nation could not afford to lose Kentucky at this crisis," the *New York Times* reported, "and gave it as his opinion that to arm the negroes would turn 50,000 bayonets from the loyal Border States against us." Hunter failed to secure pay for his regiment and in August disbanded the outfit, preserving only Company A, under Captain Charles T. Trowbridge, which camped south of Port Royal at Saint Simons Island.

Later that month, however, Brigadier General Rufus Saxton requested permission from Secretary Stanton to raise an armed force of African American soldiers, pleading that the Department of the South's shortage of soldiers and Washington's inability to send reinforcements necessitated such action. Stanton's response on August 25 represented a policy sea change—the general could "arm, equip, and receive into service of the United States such volunteers of African descent as you deem expedient, not exceeding five thousand." Arming a company of troops at Saint Simons Island, Saxton launched them on a raid up coastal rivers along the Florida-Georgia border. The mission was a success, and the outfit returned with supplies and reinforcements. He jubilantly informed Stanton, "It is admitted on all hands that the negroes fought with a coolness bravery that would have done credit to veteran soldiers."

With Company A at its core, the 1st South Carolina Regiment formally entered Federal service outside Beaufort on January 1, 1863, the same day that Lincoln's Emancipation Proclamation took effect. The new regiment's commander, Colonel Thomas Wentworth Higginson from Massachusetts, was an ardent abolitionist and a friend and admirer of John Brown. Later that month, after discarding the red pantaloons, Higginson led his men on an expedition up Saint Marys River near the Georgia-Florida border and returned with more supplies, including railroad iron, bricks, and lumber.

Saxton then authorized a second African American regiment, the 2nd South Carolina, also comprising former slaves, many of them liberated by his incursions up the tidal rivers. In January 1863, Colonel James Montgomery arrived to command the regiment and began recruiting among the freedmen. Montgomery had participated conspicuously in the bloody "Jayhawker" raids in Kansas, waging violent warfare against proslavery landowners. For him, the fight against slavery was personal; he had watched with his wife and children as proslavery guerillas burned their home to the ground. Harboring a visceral hatred of slaveholders, Montgomery determined to punish them by burning their plantations, driving them from their homes, and liberating their slaves. In March, his embryonic regiment, serving as part of Higginson's command, made a successful foray up the Saint Johns River that culminated in Jacksonville's capture and occupation. "It is my belief," General Saxton wrote Stanton, "that scarcely an incident in this war has caused greater panic throughout the whole Southern coast than this raid of the colored troops in Florida." The soldiers were soon recalled, however, out of the War Department's concern that it might need them in operations against Charleston. Higginson assessed Montgomery as "splendid, but impulsive and changeable; never plans far ahead, and goes off at a tangent." Shaw later observed that the Kansan "allows no swearing or drinking in his regiment and is anti-tobacco—but he burns and destroys wherever he goes with great gusto, and looks as if he had quite a taste for hanging people and throat-cutting whenever a suitable subject offers."

Drawing on assistance from Harriet Tubman, an escaped slave now aiding the Federal war effort in South Carolina, Hunter next directed Montgomery to launch an expedition up the Combahee River, a few miles north of Beaufort, to confiscate supplies, destroy railroads and bridges, and otherwise disrupt rebel supply lines and free the enslaved population. The 2nd South Carolina was mustered into service in late May 1863, and on June 1, Montgomery and Tubman set off in ships, along with three hundred of the colonel's African American soldiers and a company from the 3rd Rhode Island Heavy Artillery. The expedition was a resounding success. As the boats moved upriver, detachments disembarked and fanned into the countryside, seizing cotton, rice, corn, and other crops and burning plantation houses. One ship made it to Combahee Ferry, where the main road from Charleston crossed the river on a makeshift pontoon bridge. While soldiers ignited the bridge, others ventured to a nearby plantation under orders to seize any useable property and destroy whatever they could not carry off. In all, the raiders burned nine plantation homes to the ground.

Slaves rushed to the river by the hundreds and pled for permission to board. Montgomery dispatched small boats to pick them up, but pandemonium ensued as the enslaved people, desperate for freedom, tried to climb aboard, threatening to capsize the boats. Crews tried beating the slaves' hands with oars, but the frantic Blacks refused to release their hold. Tubman later left a vivid description of fugitives, baskets of food hanging from their shoulders and children on their backs, wrapped in a cacophony of squealing pigs, squawking chickens, and screaming children. She recalled a woman dragging two pigs, a white one named Beauregard and a black one named Jeff Davis. Making multiple trips, the small boats brought off more than 750 slaves. Montgomery then addressed the crowd, as did Tubman. "For sound sense and real native eloquence her address would do honor to any man, and it created a great sensation," a Boston newspaper reported.

Hunter's successful raids elevated the freedmen soldiers' mood and increased their standing with their white counterparts, who had initially doubted their Black comrades. "Our colored troops are more than a match for any equal number of White rebels which can be brought against them," a *New York Times* correspondent reported, concluding that "these free men are all-sufficient to snuff out the rebellion." In a similar vein, Saxton informed Secretary Stanton that "in every action the negro troops have behaved with the utmost bravery" and that "never in a single instance can I learn that they have flinched." Another officer who had initially harbored doubts about African American soldiers admitted that the 1st South Carolina's performance persuaded him that it was "as efficient a regiment I believe as there is in the Union army."

Colonel Montgomery's Combahee expedition, Hunter boasted to

Governor Andrew, "is but the initial step of a system of operations which will rapidly compel the Rebels to either lay down their arms and sue for restoration to the Union or to withdraw their slaves into the interior, thus leaving desolate the most fertile and productive of their counties along the Atlantic seaboard." Hunter wrote Secretary of War Stanton in the same vein, informing him that "Colonel Montgomery with his forces will repeat his incursions as rapidly as possible in different directions, injuring the enemy all he can and carrying away their slaves, thus rapidly filling up the South Carolina regiments in the department, of which there are now four."

In Confederate eyes, however, Hunter's regiments of freed slaves represented an abomination, and Southerners held that general in especially high contempt. Confederate authorities in August 1862 accused Hunter, along with Brigadier General John W. Phelps, a Union commander in Louisiana who had also championed arming former slaves, of attempting to "inaugurate a servile war" that would lead to the "indiscriminate slaughter of all ages, sexes, and conditions." The Confederate War Department went so far as to issue a general order proclaiming Hunter and Phelps "outlaws: and in the event of the capture of either of them, or that of any other officer employed in drilling and organizing slaves, with a view to their armed service in this war, shall not be regarded as a prisoner of War, but held in close confinement for execution as a felon, at such time and place as the President shall order." In April 1863, the Confederacy's president, Jefferson Davis, proclaimed that commissioned officers of the United States commanding armed former slaves were "not entitled to be considered as soldiers engaged in honorable warfare but as robbers and criminals deserving death, and that each of them be whenever captured reserved for execution." The next month, the Confederate Congress issued an even stronger mandate, resolving that "every white person being a commissioned officer ... who during the present war shall command negroes or mulattoes in arms against the Confederate States or who shall arm, train, organize or prepare negroes and mulattoes ... shall if captured be put to death or be otherwise punished at the discretion of the court."

In an unprecedented move, Hunter responded directly to President Davis, mincing no words. "You say you are fighting for liberty," he wrote the Confederate leader:

Yes you are fighting for liberty: liberty to keep four millions of your fellow-beings in ignorance and degradation;—liberty to separate parents and children, husband and wife, brother and sister;—liberty to steal the products of their labor, exacted with many a cruel lash and bitter tear;—liberty to seduce their wives and daughters, and to sell your own children into bondage;—liberty to kill these children with impunity, when the murder cannot be proven by one of pure white blood. This is the kind of liberty—the liberty to do wrong—which Satan, Chief of the fallen Angels, was contending for when he was cast into Hell.

While Swails and his fellow soldiers settled into their camp near Beaufort, Colonel Shaw caught up with Montgomery, who had just returned from the Combahee. Although Shaw judged him a "good man to begin under," he expressed reservations in a letter to his father. "He is an Indian in his mode of warfare, and though I am glad to see something of it, I can't say I admire it. It isn't like a fair stand up such as our Potomac Army is accustomed to."

Hunter, too, was beginning to harbor concerns about Montgomery's excesses, and on hearing details of the Combahee raid sent the colonel a cautionary reminder. Assuring the colonel that he in no manner doubted "the justice or generosity of your judgment," the general forwarded him a copy of the War Department's General Order No. 100, entitled "Instructions for the government of armies of the United States in the field," and directed him to "exercise the utmost strictness in insisting upon compliance with the instructions herewith sent, and you will avoid any devastation which does not strike immediately at the resources or material of the armed insurrection which we are now engaged in the task of suppressing." Hunter authorized Montgomery to "at once enroll and arm [any freed Negroes] as soldiers" and to confiscate any horses, mules, cattle, and foodstuffs that the enemy might use or that could be helpful to the Federal forces. He was to avoid, however, wanton destruction and was to spare household furniture, libraries, churches, and hospitals. In short, the colonel was to "hold the troops under your command to the very strictest interpretation of the laws and usages of civilized warfare." Whether Montgomery would adhere to Hunter's directive would shortly be tested.

At sunrise on June 8, the 54th Massachusetts marched to the wharf in Beaufort, and Swails set off once again on the *DeMolay,* gaily singing "John Brown's Body" with the rest of the regiment. Arriving at Hilton Head, Shaw was instructed to report to Montgomery at Saint Simons Island, some eighty miles south on the Georgia coast. The steamer departed that evening and reached its destination on the southern tip of Saint Simons early the next morning. At noon, another steamer—"a small craft that looked like a canal boat with a one-story house built upon it," according to one of Shaw's men—took the 54th on a ten-mile journey along the western edge of the island to Pike's Bluff, where the regiment joined Montgomery's 2nd South Carolina at its encampment. Swails and the rest of the 54th erected shelters on the edge of a clearing. Despite the heat and insects, they found the place enchanting. "The foliage is wonderfully thick, and the trees covered with hanging moss, making beautiful avenues wherever there is a road or path; it is more like the tropics than anything I have seen," Shaw wrote Annie, whom he had married shortly before leaving Boston.

The next day—June 10—a steamer drew up to Pike's Bluff carrying Colonel Montgomery. Hailing Shaw from the deck, Montgomery shouted, "How soon can you be ready to start on an expedition?" Shaw hollered back, "In half an hour," and at 6:00 P.M., eight companies from the 54th Massachusetts set off upriver. Remaining behind to guard the camp were Companies F and C. Assigned to Company F, Swails thus stayed on Saint Simons Island while the larger portion of his regiment departed for its first encounter with the enemy.

Montgomery's objective was the small town of Darien, several miles up the Altamaha River and readily accessible from Saint Simons Island. Perched on bluffs above the river, Darien was a busy commercial port where produce—chiefly cotton and timber—from the surrounding countryside was shipped out. Montgomery's force consisted of five companies from his own 2nd South Carolina, eight companies from Shaw's 54th Massachusetts, and the 3rd Rhode Island Heavy Artillery. The expedition got off to a tardy start when one ship grounded and another ran onto a shoal, but the three transports, accompanied by a navy gunboat, were well along the Altamaha by morning on June 11. "On the way up, Montgomery threw several shells among the plantation buildings, in what seemed to me a very brutal way," Shaw later wrote, "for he didn't know how many women and children there might be."

Around noon, Darien—"a beautiful little town," as Shaw described it, consisting of some eighty homes, five churches, twelve stores, a courthouse, a jail, a school, a few mills, and warehouses containing rice, turpentine, and resin—came into sight. Montgomery instructed his gunners to lob a few shells into the place as his boats made fast to the wharf and troops poured into the village. Except for two white and two Black women, the town appeared deserted, the other residents having fled. A handful of Confederates from the 20th Georgia Cavalry had been patrolling there but were also gone, leaving Darien undefended.

The Black troops thoroughly looted the town, including private residences, and returned to the ships carrying a vast array of household items, including sofas, tables, pianos, chairs, mirrors, carpets, beds, tools, books, and china. One man came back grasping several chickens in one hand and in the other hand pulling a rope with a cow attached. When the decks became too crowded to hold more livestock, soldiers shot the town's remaining cattle and horses. An elegant home surrounded by trees and flowers attracted the attention of the 54th's Captain John Appleton, who ventured inside. "Going through the house, which was well furnished, I found nothing of use in camp," he later wrote, "but Col. Shaw and myself met in one room and sadly gazed at the family portraits, etc., doomed to the flames." Shaw, he recalled, seemed "indignant at our having to burn the town, thinking that its destruction was simply under orders from Montgomery."

Once Darien had been "thoroughly disemboweled," Shaw wrote his wife the next day, Montgomery announced, "I shall burn this town." Shaw responded that he did not want the responsibility, so the Kansan gave the order, personally setting a building on fire himself. Montgomery also directed one of the Massachusetts companies to assist in the arson, leaving Shaw to conclude that he had no choice but to obey a direct order and permit his men to comply. Montgomery justified his actions by advising him that "the Southerners must be made to feel that this was a real war, and that they were to be swept away by the hand of God, like the Jews of old." He added, "We are outlawed, and therefore not bound by the rules of warfare." Shaw was not persuaded. "In theory it may seem all right to some, but when it comes to being made the instrument of the Lord's vengeance, I myself don't like it," he wrote home the next day. Montgomery's justification for vandalism, he believed, "makes it none the less revolting to wreak vengeance on the innocent and defenseless."

After the soldiers had ignited the warehouses near Darien's wharfs, the ships pulled away. "The riverbank was a sheet of flame," a Massachusetts man recalled, generating heat so intense that the troops crowded onto the far side of the boats. Only three small houses and a Methodist church remained standing afterward. Otherwise, the town, according to a resident who later surveyed the wreckage, had been reduced to "one plane of ashes and of Blackened chimneys, . . . burned in broad daylight by the cowardly Yankee-negro thieves." Another noted that Darien's destruction "afforded a safe opportunity to inflict injury upon unarmed and defenseless private citizens, and it is in such enterprises that Yankee-negro valor displays itself."

Shaw rightfully worried that the pillaging and burning of Darien would sour the public's perception of African American soldiers. "Besides my own distaste for this barbarous sort of warfare, I am not sure that it will not harm very much the reputation of Black troops and of those connected with them," he wrote his wife the next day. "For myself, I have gone through the war so far without dishonor, and I do not like to denigrate into a plunderer and robber,—and the same applies to every officer in my regiment. There was not a deed performed, from beginning to end, which required any pluck or courage. If we had fought for possession of the place, and it had been found necessary to hold or destroy it, or if the inhabitants had anything which deserved such punishment, or if it were a place of refuge for the enemy, there might have been some reason for Montgomery's acting as he did; but as the case stands, I can't see any justification." Two weeks later, as the negative reports that he had feared appeared in newspapers, Shaw wrote his wife: "I think now, as I did at the time, that it is cruel, barbarous, impolitic, and degrading to ourselves and to our men; and I shall always rejoice that I expressed myself so at the time of the destruction of Darien. It is rather hard that my men, officers, and myself should have to bear part of the abuse for the destruction of Darien, isn't it?—when they (at least the officers) all felt just as I did about it."

The 54th Massachusetts was back on Saint Simons Island the next afternoon and settled into camp on the Gould plantation. Following the controversial raid on Darien, President Lincoln decided to remove

Hunter from command of the Department of the South, tactfully informing the general that he was doing so "for no reasons which convey any
imputation upon your known energy, efficiency and patriotism; but for
causes which seemed sufficient, while they were in no degree incom-
patible with the respect and esteem in which I have always held you as
a man and officer."* His replacement was Brigadier General Quincy A.
Gillmore. A career military man and an engineer of considerable repute,
Gillmore had graduated first in his class at West Point and taught engi-
neering at the military academy. He served as chief engineer of the Port
Royal expedition in 1861 and subsequently masterminded the reduction
of Fort Pulaski, defending Savannah. The 1st South Carolina's Colonel
Higginson observed that "everyone likes and admires Gen. Gillmore
thus far—he is dashing, cordial, approachable, fair, decided and has the
prestige of success, with that immense visible activity of temperament
which always commands enthusiasm, sometimes exaggerated." He was
especially impressed by the general's "organizing as well as executive
power."

On June 24, Swails and the 54th sailed to Saint Helena Island, near
Hilton Head, where they camped beside Montgomery's 2nd South Carolina. The forces on the island, which included several regiments, were
commanded by Brigadier General George C. Strong, described by Captain
Emilio as a "brilliant young officer who had recently arrived." This was
Swails's first opportunity to interact closely with an outfit composed of
men who until recently had been enslaved. While he never recorded his
impressions, Swails must have been struck by how dramatically Montgomery's troops differed from himself and his fellow soldiers in the 54th
Massachusetts, who had spent most or all of their lives as free men in
the North.

Saint Helena Island proved a comfortable post, but Swails and the
men of the 54th were concerned that they were being sidelined. Their
concern redoubled on July 3, when Strong and his brigade—of which

---

*Hunter subsequently commanded Union forces operating in the Shenandoah Valley,
where he gained notoriety for his scorched-earth policy and burning of the Virginia Military Institute in Lexington. He later presided over the trial of the alleged conspirators
accused of killing President Lincoln. Hunter retired from the army in 1866 and lived in
Washington, DC, where he died in 1886.

the 54th Massachusetts was not a part—departed for Folly Island, near Charleston, where Union forces were girding for another try at breaching the Confederate fortifications protecting its harbor. Three days later, Colonel Shaw wrote Strong expressing regret that his regiment had not been included. "I was the more disappointed at being left behind, that I had been given to understand that we were to have our share in the work in this department," he explained. "I feel convinced too that my men are capable of better service than mere guerrilla warfare, and I hoped to remain permanently under your command." He closed by affirming his "trust that the present arrangement is not permanent."

On July 8, Shaw received encouraging news. His regiment was to join the forces assembling for an offensive against Charleston, the men taking only blankets and rations. The waiting was over, and Sergeant Swails was about to have his first taste of combat.

CHAPTER THREE

Looking Out from among the Ghastly Corpses

From the North's perspective, Charleston was an attractive prize. The city served not only as a major seaport and transportation hub but also as the seat of the rebellion, where secession first found concrete expression and where the war's first shots were fired. In 1862, Federal forces launched a major offensive against the "Holy City"—as Charleston, its skyline bristling with church spires, was sometimes called—but that attempt had failed. Now the Department of the South's new chief, General Gillmore, determined to try once again.

The key to taking Charleston, Gillmore concluded, involving neutralizing Fort Sumter, a commanding edifice at the mouth of Charleston Harbor whose artillery prevented Union ships from reaching the city. To accomplish that goal, the general proposed capturing Morris Island, a small spit of land on the harbor's southern edge, from where the Federals could bombard Fort Sumter, force its surrender, and then clear the harbor of obstructions and capture Charleston. Confederates presently occupied Morris Island and had constructed two forts there. Undeterred, Gillmore reasoned that he could take the island with a joint attack by gunboats and infantry.

In early June 1863, Gillmore refined his strategy. The general boasted impressive credentials in these matters, as he had led the Union offensive fourteen months earlier that had captured Fort Pulaski. This time, he decided to begin with two diversionary movements aimed at misleading the Confederates and drawing enemy troops away from his true target. He directed Colonel Higginson to take the 1st South Carolina up the Edisto River and threaten the Charleston and Savannah Railroad, hopefully cutting the line at the tiny settlement of Jacksonborough. Simultaneously, he tasked Brigadier General Alfred Terry's division to proceed up the

Stono River and feign an attack against the city from nearby James Island. Brigadier General Truman Seymour's division, with Strong's brigade in the lead, would execute the operation's critical element—the main attack against Morris Island—by massing on Folly Island, crossing Lighthouse Inlet onto the southern tip of Morris, regrouping, and then pushing northward to overrun Forts Wagner and Gregg on the island's northern end as Union warships bombarded those bastions with heavy cannon fire.

General Pierre Gustave Toutant Beauregard, commanding the Confederate forces protecting Charleston, accurately predicted the likely Union offensive. "The James Island line is their best; but that is very strong," he wrote. "I think it's more probable they will move from Stono Inlet along Folly Island, thence Morris Island, to endeavor to take Fort Sumter a la [Fort] Pulaski." Beauregard meant to be prepared and set about strengthening Wagner and Gregg. As he quipped, the general intended for the Federals to discover their Folly Island offensive "to be a piece of Folly."

By early July, Beauregard had fashioned Fort Wagner—named after Lieutenant Colonel Thomas M. Wagner, killed at Fort Moultrie on the opposite side of the harbor—into an imposing fortification. Constructed of earth, sand, and palmetto logs, one of its sloping faces rose 30 feet and extended 635 feet across the island's sandy width, from the Atlantic Ocean on the east to an impassable marsh on the west. Armed with six artillery pieces, the edifice blocked any Union advance by land toward Morris Island's northern tip. A second face, mounting three artillery pieces, looked to the ocean to repel any naval attack. A huge salient connected the two faces, and an earthen wall extended across the island, providing an additional obstacle to any force attacking by land. Workers also dug a moat in front of the fort, 10 feet wide and 5 feet deep, which filled with seawater at high tide and completed the defenses across the island's narrow neck. Nestled inside Wagner were magazines, living quarters, and a large protected bunker to shelter the occupants during bombardments. Captain Emilio, who experienced Wagner firsthand, later termed it "the strongest single earthwork known in the history of warfare." Fort Gregg loomed north of Wagner on Cummings Point. Shielded by Wagner from any land attack, it was lightly manned and equipped to fire on ships seeking entry into Charleston Harbor.

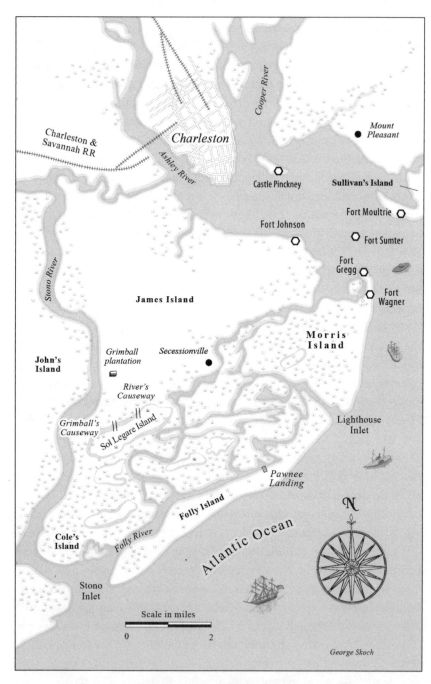

Charleston & Savannah RR

Charleston

Ashley River

Cooper River

Mount Pleasant

Castle Pinckney

Sullivan's Island

Fort Moultrie

Fort Johnson

Fort Sumter

Stono River

Fort Gregg

Fort Wagner

James Island

Morris Island

Grimball plantation

Secessionville

John's Island

River's Causeway

Grimball's Causeway

Sol Legare Island

Lighthouse Inlet

Pawnee Landing

Folly Island

Cole's Island

Folly River

Atlantic Ocean

N

Stono Inlet

Scale in miles

0   2

George Skoch

Theater of the 54th Massachusetts's Operations near Charleston

During the night of July 8, transports carrying the 54th Massachu-setts from Saint Helena Island started north up the coast. A thunder-storm exacerbated the voyage's discomfort, drenching Swails and his fellow passengers and subjecting them to several miserable hours of gut-wrenching pitching about in the crowded steamers. Shortly after midnight, the seasick soldiers steamed into the Stono River, already packed with transports, gunboats, and supply vessels preparing for Gill-more's imminent assault against Morris Island. There the ships carrying the 54th dropped anchor off Folly Island's southern tip.

That afternoon, following Gillmore's grand plan, Terry's division launched its diversion, proceeding up the Stono River and deploying on Battery and Sol Legare Islands, immediately adjacent to James Island, to feign an attack toward Charleston. Meanwhile, Higginson, leading the other diversionary expedition, left Beaufort with the 1st South Carolina and an artillery section and headed up the South Edisto River toward Jacksonborough. Before reaching his objective—the Charleston and Savanah Railroad bridge—Higginson's transports ran aground, forcing him to abandon the venture. A soldier who took part in the abortive raid noted that they had destroyed a few hundred bushels of rice, burned a mill, captured a lieutenant and two men, and liberated two hundred slaves. The railroad, however, remained intact and in service for the Confederates.

Near sunrise on July 10, Swails and his fellow soldiers, still on trans-ports in Stono Inlet, heard heavy cannonading from the direction of Morris Island. That evening, they received word that Seymour's Federals had overrun the island up to Fort Wagner. Heartening news also arrived from other theaters of the war. General Robert E. Lee's Army of North-ern Virginia had been defeated at Gettysburg, and Vicksburg had fallen to Major General Ulysses S. Grant's Federals.

The next day, the 54th Massachusetts's transports carried the soldiers two miles up the Stono River to join Terry's men, some of whom had camped at the Grimball plantation on a finger of land jutting into the Stono, with pickets extending southeastward onto nearby Sol Legare Island, where the general's main body was located. Swails and the rest of his regiment disembarked on Sol Legare and manned part of a Union picket line in conjunction with white soldiers from the 10th Connecti-cut. Meanwhile, surmising that the Confederates had likely weakened their defenses on Morris Island by dispatching troops to counter Terry's threat, Gillmore had launched a major assault against Fort Wagner. The defenders repelled this attack with ease, inflicting 339 Union casualties in contrast to only 12 casualties for the Southerners.

Over the next few days, Terry's front remained quiet. On Sol Legare, the 54th Massachusetts saw little activity. Swails and the other soldiers rotated on picket duty, with three or four of the regiment's ten companies assigned to the line each day. Living conditions were miserable. "We have not had our clothes off since we left St. Helena, and have absolutely nothing but an India rubber blanket apiece," Shaw wrote home. "Officers and men are in the same boat." The inhospitable terrain added to the men's discomfort. This coastal region, known as the Low Country, consisted of muddy marshland that flooded at high tide. Slightly higher pockets of land were accessible only along tidal creeks by boat or by slogging through deep mud when the tide fell sufficiently low. In places, enterprising plantation owners had built bridges or causeways across the mudflats to connect the islands. Such was the situation on Sol Legare, joined to larger James Island by causeways. Surrounded by marsh, Swails and his companions sweltered under the brutal summer sun and waged a losing battle against insects.

On the evening of July 15, Companies B, H, and K occupied the 54th's picket line facing north toward the marshy creek separating Sol Legare and James Islands. Captain William H. Simpkins, a white officer who had given "much hard thinking" before agreeing to serve in a Black regiment, commanded the 54th's pickets this evening. "Lurking men were seen" on the marsh's far bank, Captain Emilio recalled, "occasional shots rang out," and signal lights flashed in the dark, suggesting that a Confederate offensive was imminent. Captain Simpkins directed the pickets to lie down and seek cover, instructing several of them to hunker behind a hedge.

The rebels were indeed preparing to attack. Brigadier General Alfred H. Colquitt was girding to cross River's Causeway over the marsh separating James Island from Sol Legare, roll up Shaw's pickets, and then cross back along another causeway closer to the Stono River that would bring him behind Terry's soldiers at the Grimball place. A second Confederate force, under Colonel Charlton S. Way, stood poised to attack the Grimball plantation from the north to crush the Federals there in a pincer movement formed by his and Colquitt's offensives. At the same time, Confederate artillery planned to open fire on Union gunboats in the Stono.

Fighting erupted at dawn on July 16 as Confederate artillery began shelling Simpkins's picket line. An officer in the 54th vaulted onto a stack of empty cracker boxes and spotted flashes of musketry across the marsh, signaling that the Confederate attack was underway. Then came the pounding roar of cannon as rebel artillery opened up on Union ships in the Stono near the Grimball plantation. The river channel there was narrow, preventing the craft from turning and responding to the enemy fire.

On Sol Legare Island, Shaw directed the rest of his regiment, including Swails's company, to deploy to the right and rear of Simpkins's picket line, where they could control River's Causeway. Swails and his companions heard hoarse commands in Southern accents, and suddenly Colquitt's Confederates burst through the morning mist, heading directly toward them.

This was the 54th Massachusetts's baptism by fire, and the Black soldiers performed spectacularly, fully meeting Shaw's expectations. As Colquitt's foremost elements materialized, the 54th's pickets rose and fired into the approaching troops. "That was something the rebels didn't expect," a soldier in the 54th wrote, "their line of skirmishers was completely broken; our men then began to fall back gradually on our line of battle, as the rebels were advancing their main force on them." Individual acts of bravery were legion. African American Sergeant James D. Wilson, reputedly a crack shot, had repeatedly promised his comrades that he would never retreat or surrender; he proved as good as his word. Standing fast, he repelled an attack by five Confederates, killing three of them, and held off a cluster of circling cavalrymen with his bayonet until he fell dead, his body pierced by multiple bullets.

Massively outnumbered, Shaw's troops, including Swails, retarded but could not halt Colquitt's advance. The 54th Massachusetts's determined fighting, however, bought time for the 10th Connecticut's pickets next to them to withdraw and rejoin Terry's main body. A Union newspaper correspondent later reported that the "boys of the Tenth Connecticut could not help loving the men who saved them from destruction." He was deeply touched, the correspondent continued, "at hearing this feeling expressed by officers and men of the Connecticut regiment; and probably a thousand homes from Windham to Fairfield have in letter been told the story how these dark-skinned heroes fought the good fight and covered with their own brave hearts the retreat of brothers, sons, and fathers of Connecticut."

The time gained by the determined stand of Swails and his fellow soldiers on Sol Legare also permitted Terry's main body to prepare to receive the Confederate onslaught. The 54th regrouped on the island, "all bearing evidence of struggles with bush and brier," Captain Emilio recalled, "some of the wounded limping along unassisted, others helped by comrades." Captain Simpkins came in last, uninjured but with his trousers and coat punctured by multiple bullets. Meanwhile, the Union gunboats in the Stono finally managed to shift into position and took up the challenge, joined by artillery from two armed transports in Folly Creek on the Federal right flank. Facing unexpected resistance, the Confederates called off their attack and retired.

In his report on the James Island operation, General Terry remarked on "the steadiness and soldierly conduct of the Fifty-fourth Massachusetts Regiment, who were on duty at the outposts on the right, and met the brunt of the attack." Troops from the 10th Connecticut visited the 54th Massachusetts's camp to thank the men who had saved them, and soldiers from other outfits echoed the same sentiment. "It is not for us to blow our horn," one of Swails's compatriots wrote, "but when a regiment of white men gave us three cheers as we were passing them, it shows that we did our duty as men should." Scrawled another proud African American warrior: "For the first time colored men had been hand to hand with the enemy, and their stubborn courage filled the officers with joy." That evening, Shaw wrote home that the praise was "very gratifying to us personally, and a fine thing for the coloured troops. It is the first time that they have been associated with white soldiers, this side of the Mississippi." He closed by observing, "I know this letter will give you pleasure, because what we have done today wipes out the memory of the Darien affair, which you could not but grieve over, though we were innocent participators."

In all, the 54th lost fourteen soldiers killed, eighteen wounded, and thirteen missing, totaling forty-five casualties. It initially appeared that some of the regiment's fallen had been mutilated, although it was ultimately determined that fiddler crabs, which proliferated in the marshy terrain, had mauled the bodies. Shaw received conflicting reports concerning how the Confederates had treated their African American captives; some said that the rebels treated them well, while others reported that they shot several prisoners.

At sunset, Terry began withdrawing to Folly Island. The troops at the Grimball plantation had the easiest time of it, boarding transports that took them down the Stono River to Folly Island. The soldiers on Sol Legare—the 54th Massachusetts, the 2nd South Carolina, and the 10th Connecticut—took a different route, working due south across sodden marshland. Swails and his companions started walking at 9:40 that night through a marsh to Cole's Island, then headed toward Folly River, where they expected boats to take them across to Folly Island. Swails would never forget the ordeal. Rain lashed, thunder roared, wind howled, and the pace was agonizingly slow as he and the other soldiers of the 54th slogged single file along a muddy path, clods of dirt clinging to their boots. "For nearly half a mile we had to pass over a bridge of one, and in some places, two planks wide, without a railing, and slippery with rain," recalled Shaw, who led the march, "and then over a narrow dike so slippery as to make it almost impossible to keep one's feet." Captain Emilio reported that the soldiers crept carefully along, "groping their way and grasping their leaders as they progressed, that they might not separate or go astray." Swails and his companions were frequently forced to pause until lightening lit the path. Wrote Shaw, "I never had such an extraordinary walk."

Finally, near daybreak, the 54th's lead elements emerged onto a beach facing Folly Island. No food or water was available, and many of the troops had eaten nothing for over a day. Swails and his fellow soldiers collapsed on the beach and fell fast asleep under the blistering sun, expecting transports to arrive and take them across the river. When a single boat named *General Hunter* appeared at eight that night, they could scarcely believe their eyes. The only way to reach the craft was by way of a leaky longboat that held no more than thirty men. All night, buffeted by another raging storm, the longboat circled back and forth between the shore and the *General Hunter,* ferrying more than a thousand soldiers, thirty at a time. At daylight the next morning, the loading complete, Colonel Shaw boarded with the last group.

The steamer ran up Folly River and at 9:00 A.M., June 18, reached Pawnee Landing, where the 54th disembarked and marched across Folly Island to its beach-lined eastern edge. "Well done! We heard your guns," soldiers shouted as Swails and the other weary troops passed. "Hurrah, boys! You saved the Tenth Connecticut!" Continuing up the beach, the men of the 54th reached Lighthouse Inlet, where they boarded a small steamer that took them across to Morris Island, landing them there—still without food—at 5:00 P.M.

A furious onslaught by Gillmore's land-based artillery and Rear Admiral John A. Dahlgren's warships and ironclads had been pounding Fort Wagner all day. Its commander, Brigadier General William B. Taliaferro, estimated that approximately 9,000 projectiles slammed into Wagner, nearly one shell every two seconds, in perhaps the most concentrated artillery barrage of the Civil War. "Words cannot depict the thunder, the smoke, the lifted sand and the general havoc," reported Taliaferro. "The whole island smoked like a furnace and trembled as from an earthquake." To Gillmore and his officers, the sustained bombardment seemed to have battered the fort into submission. Troops no longer appeared atop Wagner's parapets, suggesting that the shelling had decimated the garrison and disabled the cannon. It was time, the general concluded, to bring Wagner to its knees with a final, irresistible charge directly up the beach.

General Seymour, who Gillmore selected to oversee the assault, decided to send Strong's brigade in first, followed if necessary by Colonel Haldimand S. Putnam's and Brigadier General Thomas G. Stevenson's brigades. Putnam, who had been Strong's classmate at West Point, had serious reservations about the attack. "We are all going into Wagner like a flock of sheep," he remarked. "Seymour is a devil of a fellow for dash."

Together, Seymour and Strong selected the 54th Massachusetts to spearhead the attack. The reason for their choice has aroused heated debate. In February 1864, *New York Tribune* correspondent Nathaniel Paige professed to have overheard Gillmore and Seymour discussing which troops to put in front. "Well I guess we will let Strong lead and put those damned niggers from Massachusetts in the advance," he claimed to have heard Seymour recommend. "We may as well get rid of them one time as another." In his after-action report, Seymour gave a different explanation for his decision, observing that the "Fifty-fourth

Massachusetts, a colored regiment of excellent character, well officered, with full ranks, and that had conducted itself commendably a few days previously on James Island, was placed in front." He later elaborated that "it was believed that the Fifty-fourth was in every respect as efficient as any other body of men; and as it was one of the strongest and best officered, there seemed to be no good reason why it should not be selected for the advance." We will never know Strong's version of why he and Seymour selected the 54th Massachusetts to lead the attack, as he died during the action.

Gillmore clearly believed that Fort Wagner was doomed. He failed to recognize, however, that while the pounding had indeed badly scarred the bastion, its sand-and-palmetto-log construction had absorbed the artillery's punishment and preserved the fort's defensive capacity. Confederate losses were surprisingly minor, and the bombardment did little more than alert the defenders that a Federal infantry attack was imminent. The foremost Union troops, whoever they might be, would be marching into a killing field.

Shortly after arriving on Morris Island, Shaw and his adjutant, Garth W. James, conferred with Brigadier General Strong, who informed them that they were to storm Fort Wagner that evening. Doubtless recalling the colonel's letter to him a few days earlier boasting that his men were "capable of better service than mere guerrilla warfare," Strong looked Shaw in the eye and announced, "You may lead the column, if you say 'yes.'" To clarify that the final decision was up to him, the general added: "Your men, I know, are worn out, but do as you choose." According to James, Shaw's face brightened, and he ordered the adjutant to inform Lieutenant Colonel Hallowell to bring the 54th to the front. Swails and the rest of the regiment were soon marching by, and Strong, "noticing the worn look of the men, who had passed two days without an issue of rations, and no food since morning, when the weary march began . . . , expressed his sympathy and his great desire that they might have food and stimulant," James recalled. The time set for the attack had arrived, however, and the weary soldiers continued to the front.

At 6:30 P.M., Shaw and Strong rode to the head of the 54th Massachusetts. On the way, the colonel handed some personal papers to a friend, asking that he pass them on to his family should he fail to return. Once he had positioned his troops, Shaw directed them to lie down, muskets loaded and bayonets fixed. Stretched out on the sand, Sergeant Swails watched as dense sea fog collected in the east, and the setting sun brightened the western sky. Distant thunder and the roar of cannon interrupted his revelries, and as he looked back, his gaze settled on the silent lines of troops stretching to the rear, parting only briefly to let horsemen carrying orders pass through to the front. "All was ominous of the impending onslaught," a fellow onlooker reflected. Captain Appleton recalled that the soldiers spoke in "low tones with each other," telling their comrades "where our letters were in our pockets and asked that they be sent home in case we did not come out of the fight."

It was clear that the assault would not be easy. The 54th Massachusetts stood some 1,300 yards south of Fort Wagner. The attack route ran along a narrow strip of deep, loose sand little more than 100 yards wide, hemmed in on one side by the ocean and on the other by marshes and brush. Near Wagner, the marsh intruded toward the ocean, creating a narrow defile through which the attacking force would have to funnel, offering the Confederates a tightly packed target. After that came the fort's outer wall, which would have to be scaled; its moat, which would have to be crossed; and then its main wall and battlements, which would have to be mounted, all of these obstacles retarding the attacking troops and keeping them under the enemy's killing fire.

As the moment approached, General Strong, mounted on a gray charger and splendidly outfitted in full dress, wearing white gloves and a yellow bandana coiled around his neck, rode in front of the regiment, shouted words of encouragement, and advised: "Don't fire a musket on the way up, but go in and bayonet them at their guns." Taking the flag from the regiment's color bearer, he waved the banner aloft, and the soldiers cheered. "If this man should fall, who will lift the flag and carry it on?" the general asked. Shaw, who was standing nearby, removed a cigar from his mouth and answered in a bold voice, "I will." Whether or not Seymour's and Strong's motive for placing the Black regiment in front involved a desire to get rid of "those damned niggers" or to afford the North's premier African American outfit a well-earned opportunity to burnish its laurels, Shaw clearly welcomed the chance for his soldiers to conclusively prove their mettle. Swails and his fellow warriors were ready to show that they could rise to the occasion.

At 7:45, with night rapidly closing in, Shaw strode before the 54th Massachusetts and shouted, "Attention!" Swails and his companions sprang immediately to their feet, brushing the sand from their uniforms. "Move in quick time until within a hundred yards of the fort," Shaw directed, "then double quick, and charge!" After an ominous pause, the colonel called out, "Forward!" and stepped off at the head of his regiment, brandishing a sword.

Wagner rose ahead, across three-quarters of a mile of sand. Squeezed into the narrow avenue between marsh and ocean, Swails and his fellow soldiers pressed tightly together, "cheering as if going on some mirthful errand." The men on the right of the line sloshed through water up to their knees, while those on the left, where Swails and Company F were positioned, tried to avoid the mud and marsh hemming them in. "The center only had a free path," Captain Emilio recounted, "and with eyes strained upon the colonel and the flag, they pressed on toward the work, now only two hundred yards away."

Until now, Wagner had loomed as an imposing but quiet presence. Suddenly a sheet of flame lit the parapet's upper margin, and musketry and artillery fire lashed the approaching soldiers. Swails pressed forward as men fell around him and explosions created huge craters in the sand. Undeterred, he and his soldiers quickened their pace, "with set jaws, panting breath, and bowed heads," one of them later recalled. A quiet of perhaps five seconds followed. "It was the calm that precedes the reloading," Adjutant James recollected. "To every soul in that surging column it must have seemed an eternity!" Soon the foremost men, Swails among them, clambered over the wall, into the ditch, and up the steep slant of the fort's shell-scarred face, the summit lined with defenders firing pointblank down at them. As Lieutenant Colonel Hallowell later reported, "Exposed to the direct fire of canister and musketry, and, as the ramparts were mounted, to a like fire on our flanks, the havoc made upon our ranks was very great."

Still leading his regiment, Colonel Shaw mounted the rampart, stood tall, raised his sword high, and shouted, "Forward, Fifty-fourth!" Sheets of bullets cut him down, killing him, but his men kept coming, many of them gaining the crest and engaging the rebel defenders in hand-to-hand combat. "The garrison fought with muskets, handspikes, and gun-rammers, the officers striking with their swords, so close were the combatants," a participant recalled. "Men fell every moment during the brief struggle. Some of the wounded crawled down the slope to shelter; others fell headlong into the ditch below."

Overwhelmed, many of Shaw's soldiers sought cover against Wagner's outer face, shooting up the exterior slope at the rebels, who in turn rolled hand grenades and burning artillery shells down on them. Confederate fire decimated the 54th's officer cadre, and when Lieutenant Colonel Hallowell fell wounded, Captain Emilio became the senior officer of rank. As the 54th's soldiers dribbled back, Emilio stationed them in an abandoned trench, where they huddled in anxious expectation of a counterattack from the rebels. The regiment's survivors included Private William H. Carney, who carried the American flag back after being twice wounded, a feat that led to his becoming the first African American to receive the Medal of Honor.

Swails was in the thick of the fighting. He, Captain Simpkins, and Captain Cabot J. Russell had gathered under the fort's main wall, climbed to the top of the parapet, and come under heavy musket fire from the defenders. Captain Russell—a nineteen-year-old former Harvard student—immediately fell wounded. Simpkins offered to have him carried back to safety, but Russell insisted on staying and asked them to straighten him out where he lay. Simpkins knelt over his head and grasped his shoulders while Swails assisted by reaching for Russell's feet, his back to the Confederates. Suddenly a musket ball tore into Simpkins's chest, killing him immediately, and he sprawled lifelessly across Russell. Swails turned and attempted to fire at the rebel shooting at them, but his musket only made a snapping sound, so he threw it down, picked up a gun belonging to a private who had just been shot, and discharged a round at the Confederate. The man dropped, and Russell implored Swails to stop shooting, fearing that it would only draw more fire from the rebels. Swails worked his way back some twenty feet, where he remained until officers ordered the regiment to retire. "It would have been impossible to have attempted to have brought either of the officers away," Swails later wrote, "for I had not the strength, nor could I have done it exposed as I was to the continued fire and hand grenades. I consider it a miracle that I myself escaped alive."

Undeterred by the defenders' overwhelming show of force, Seymour kept pushing soldiers into the fracas. The rest of Strong's brigade, following behind Shaw's regiment, attacked in two waves, the second led by the general himself, who was seriously wounded in the thigh and died a few weeks later. His men met a fate similar to that suffered by the 54th Massachusetts. "The genius of Dante could but faintly portray the horrors of that hell of fire and sulphurous smoke," recounted Elbridge J. Copp of the 3rd New Hampshire, "the agonizing shrieks of those wounded from bayonet thrust, or pierced by the bullet of the rifle, or crushed by fragments of exploring shell, sinking to earth a mass of quivering flesh and blood in the agony of horrible death." Tubman, the former slave who had become a notable spokesperson for the cause of African American liberation, put it more poetically. "And then we saw the lightning, and that was the guns," she later described the assault. "And then we heard the rain falling, and that was the drops of blood falling; and when we came to get in the crops, it was dead men that we reaped."

Seymour instructed Putnam to advance his brigade, but the colonel, dubious about the venture from the start, declined, citing an order he had received from Gillmore to stay put. He finally relented and agreed to jump into the fray after what Seymour described as "a painful and unnecessary interval." Joined by some of the 54th's survivors, the colonel managed to wedge a portion of his command into Wagner. Seymour called for more support, but before reinforcements could arrive, Confederate fire killed Putnam, and Seymour fell wounded. The general then sent his aide to bring up Stevenson's brigade, but Gillmore countermanded that order, as he did not want to commit his last remaining strength to what looked like a slaughter. Receiving no reinforcements, Putnam's survivors abandoned their foothold in Wagner and joined the retreat.

The battle ended by 10:30 that night. The attempt to take Fort Wagner had failed. In a rancorous after-action report, Seymour remarked that "what had been so dearly bought was abandoned to the enemy." The offensive's failure, he wrote, "must be ascribed solely to the unfortunate delay that hindered Colonel Putnam from moving promptly in obedience to my orders, and to his not being supported after he had essentially succeeded in the assault." Those delays, of course, had been occasioned by Gillmore, who at first thought that additional troops were unnecessary, and then, as the Confederates decimated Strong's and Putnam's brigades, decided against risking the destruction of his only remaining brigade. Seymour took care in his report not to ascribe fault to his superior, but he clearly felt that Gillmore's meddling in his attack caused the catastrophe. His anger would bear bitter fruit a few months hence, during the Florida expedition, and Swails and the 54th Massachusetts would suffer greatly because of it.

Around one o'clock in the morning—five hours after Shaw's soldiers had stepped forward at the head of the assault—the 10th Connecticut relieved the 54th Massachusetts. As the Black troops marched to the rear, guards assigned to prevent straggling accosted them. Many of those guards, one of Swails's fellow soldiers later claimed, had "imbibed rather freely," and several men of the 54th were "murdered by these drunken wretches." According to one account, a guard killed a sergeant in the 54th in front of an officer, who in turn shot the guard.

Making their way to a sand mound toward the southern end of Morris Island, Swails and the tattered remains of the 54th bivouacked for the night. While the exhausted soldiers slept, Brigadier General Stevenson, who since Seymour's and Strong's woundings had assumed command of the Union front, sent a party across the battlefield to recover any injured soldiers still living. He gave special instructions to rescue as many wounded Black troops as possible, stating, "You know how much harder they will fare at the hands of the enemy than white men." The rescue party slowly made its way to Fort Wagner, crawling through the sand and alert for the cries of the wounded. They worked until daylight made it impossible to continue, bringing back many of the wounded, including a lieutenant from the 54th.

Northern casualties were severe. Some 5,000 blue-clad soldiers had participated in the assault; of those, 246 were killed, 890 were wounded, and 391 were captured, yielding a total casualty count of 1,515 men. The 54th Massachusetts lost approximately 270 of its 600 men who went into battle, almost half of its numbers. Many wounded soldiers, unable to move, not even crawl, drowned when the tide rose. First light the next morning revealed a horrific tableau of "blood, mud, water, brains and human hair melted together; men lying in every possible attitude, with every conceivable expression on their countenances; their limbs bent into unnatural shapes by the fall of twenty or more feet; the fingers rigid and outstretched, as if they had clutched at the earth to save themselves; pale beseeching faces, looking out from among the ghastly corpses with moans and cries for help and water, and dying gasps and death struggles." A newspaper correspondent who viewed the scene concluded that "probably no battlefield in the country has ever presented such an array of mangled bodies in a small compass."

The Union high command's fatal underestimation of Fort Wagner's strength and its failure to coordinate the attacking forces doomed the offensive. As a modern student of the campaign accurately concluded, "Overconfidence, poor preparation, too much space and time between units, and the confusion caused by a night assault all led the Federals to suffer one of the war's greatest disasters." Indeed, the only Union regiment to emerge with its reputation enhanced was the 54th Massachusetts. "I saw them fight at Wagner as none but splendid soldiers, splendidly officered, could fight," wrote a *New York Herald* correspondent, "dashing through shot and shell, grape, canister, and shrapnel, and showers of bullets, and when they got close enough, fighting with clubbed muskets, and retreating when they did retreat, by command and with choice white troops for company."

As far as Swails and his fellow soldiers were concerned, Fort Wagner demonstrated that Black soldiers could fight as well as the best of their white counterparts. Even the Confederates were impressed. "The negroes fought gallantly, and were headed by as brave a colonel who ever lived," Confederate lieutenant Iredell Jones later remarked. The *New York Tribune* prophetically observed that the 54th Massachusetts's performance "made Fort Wagner such a name for the colored race as Bunker Hill has been for ninety years to the white Yankees."

Clara Barton, who had volunteered to help care for injured soldiers in South Carolina, described Morris Island as a cemetery. "The thousand little sand-hills that in the pale moonlight are a thousand headstones, and the restless ocean waves that roll and breakup on the whitened beach sing an eternal requiem to the toll-worn gallant dead who sleep beside," she wrote.

The trench in front of Wagner overflowed with bodies from the 54th Massachusetts. Confederates removed Shaw's uniform and buried the colonel in a trench alongside the corpses of twenty of the Black soldiers he had lead, apparently intending to dishonor him. On learning of his son's last resting place, Shaw's father wrote the 54th's regimental surgeon that, while he and his wife "mourn over our own loss and that of the regiment, . . . [w]e would not have his body removed from where it lies surrounded by his brave and devoted soldiers." As he explained to General Gillmore: "We hold that a soldier's most appropriate burial-place is on the field where he has fallen. I shall therefore be much obliged, General, if in case this matter is brought to your cognizance, you will forbid the desecration of my son's grave, and prevent the disturbance of his remains or those buried with him."

CHAPTER FOUR

Why Can't We Have a Soldier's Pay?

June 19—the day after the assault on Fort Wagner—"was the saddest in the history of the Fifty-fourth," Captain Emilio later wrote. Swails and the rest of the regiment waited anxiously for word of their missing comrades. Soldiers who had sought shelter elsewhere on the battlefield showed up sporadically throughout the day, but by evening, it was reasonably certain that those unaccounted for were either dead or captured. Slightly wounded men who made it back received care in camp, while those with serious wounds went to Beaufort for treatment.

The next day the regiment became part of a newly organized brigade under General Stevenson, where it served along with the 10th Connecticut and three other white regiments. Over the next six weeks, Gillmore, with naval support, prosecuted a siege operation against Fort Wagner by constructing a series of earthworks connected by zig-zag approaches for the troops, each successive entrenched position advancing closer to Wagner. Swails and his fellow soldiers in the 54th Massachusetts engaged primarily in work details, helping dig and construct entrenchments, fill and stack sandbags, and transport siege material, ordnance, and quartermaster stores to the front. Towing carts loaded with heavy guns and tons of powder and shells through soft, deep sand, often under cover of darkness, was backbreaking labor, rendered even more stressful by artillery and sniper fire from the rebels. "The faces and forms of all showed plainly at what cost this labor was done," Captain Emilio observed. "Clothes were in rags, shoes worn out, and haversacks full of holes."

On July 21, the 54th helped construct the first stage of the siege line—an entrenchment called a "parallel," its right end anchored on the ocean and the trench extending a few hundred yards across the beach to the marsh on the left. Located 1,300 yards south of Fort Wagner, this first parallel occupied essentially the same position as the jumping-off point for the big assault three days earlier. Swails and his fellow soldiers completed the second parallel 400 yards in front of the first one during the night of July 23. Connected to the first by zig-zag trenches to protect the troops from enemy fire, the second bristled with light artillery for defense and heavier ordnance to pound the rebel fort. Out of concern for the safety of the soldiers wielding picks and shovels, work proceeded mostly at night.

The next day, Colonel Milton S. Littlefield of the 4th South Carolina, another Black regiment, succeeded Captain Emilio as commander of the 54th Massachusetts. Swails and his comrades were dissatisfied; they viewed Emilio as one of them, while they knew nothing about the colonel, even though he hailed from Massachusetts. Speculation held that Littlefield received the appointment because his regiment was small and still recruiting, and he deserved a command commensurate with his rank. Within a month, however, Littlefield had won the 54th's confidence. "Few men are more capable of active, vigorous service," the soldier and correspondent George Stephens wrote in early September, "or have a higher appreciation of the services and efficiency of colored soldiers."

Work began on the third parallel and its related zig-zags on August 9. The interval between marsh and ocean at this location had narrowed to about a hundred yards, which made for a shorter entrenchment that nevertheless exposed Swails and his companions to unrelenting fire from Confederate sharpshooters. The days and nights were sweltering, no rain had fallen since July 18, and dust and sand seemed everywhere, blinding the men and coating everything in their camp. A brutal infestation of flies, sand fleas, and rats added to the torment, topped off by fevers and other diseases native to the hot, swampy environment. Soldiers fell sick at an alarming rate, and the sight of so many pale, feeble troops took a toll on morale. Barton, who also fell ill while nursing the soldiers, wrote that each man labored "sixteen hours in twenty-four in the midst of fire and death to hold the enemy back—twenty-four hours, that he could not raise his head erect once, could only be relieved under cover of darkness, and all this with a little piece of salt meat and four wormy crackers in his pocket and a canteen of warm water." A captain in the 55th Massachusetts, which had arrived on August 5, confirmed that "the little sand flies with white mugs and black heads are about as enthusiastic insects in the way of biting as they make down here." The drinking water, he added, was "perfectly horrible, being impregnated with sulfur and other southern elements."

During the night of August 21, Black soldiers completed the fourth parallel, advancing Gillmore's front to within 350 yards of Wagner. By now, Swails and his fellow troops had become accustomed to the drill. During the day, two men kept watch on Wagner and its subsidiary batteries. Whenever they spied a puff of smoke, they shouted, "Cover!" and the workers would throw down their tools, jump into the trench, and wait for the inevitable explosion. At night, lookouts could better gauge a shell's trajectory from the track of its burning fuse and limited their warning calls to only those sparking projectiles that posed a risk. Most dreaded were mortar shells, which curved into the sky, paused at their zenith, and dropped into the entrenchments, exploding and raining deadly fragments on all below. Rebel sharpshooters added to the misery and rendered failing to stay in the entrenchments certain death.

On August 24, the 54th Massachusetts joined a new brigade under Colonel Montgomery, consisting also of the 2nd South Carolina and a fresh Black regiment, the 3rd United States Colored Troops (USCT). The next evening, Union troops overran a sandy ridge in front of the fourth parallel, advancing the Federal line to within two hundred yards of Wagner. There they constructed a fifth parallel and, over the next several days, brought up more artillery and built posts for sharpshooters. At Gillmore's instruction, several powerful calcium lights illuminated Wagner to enable Union gunners to fire effectively at night and to blind the fort's defenders. On the last day of August, the 54th Massachusetts began a "special duty in the trenches" under the supervision of Major Thomas B. Brooks of the 1st New York Volunteer Engineers. Swails and the regiment relieved the 3rd USCT, which had been performing fatigue duty in the front trenches for the past ten days, "it being desirable to have older troops for the important and hazardous duty required at this period," Brooks wrote.

As September dawned, the 54th helped extend the foremost works, constantly harassed by fire from Wagner's artillery and sharpshooters. The rebels had filled the sandy expanse directly in front of the fort

with torpedoes—land mines, in modern parlance—that proved especially treacherous. "It is a duty of the greatest danger," the correspondent
Stephens wrote to Governor Andrew, "but the labor must be done, and I
feel proud that we are thus honored with the post of danger."

On September 5, Union gunboats opened a massive bombardment
that continued for forty-two hours, enabling the 54th to advance the
Union front to within a hundred yards of Wagner. Shelling intensified
the next day, both from land and sea, blasting gaps in the fort's walls
and showering dirt and debris over the entrances to its magazines and
shelters. Sensing that Wagner had reached its breaking point, Gillmore
ordered an offensive for 9:00 the next morning, when low tide would
afford the attacking troops the broadest possible approach.

Beauregard, it developed, had reached the same conclusion as Gillmore. Recognizing that he could no longer successfully defend Wagner,
he ordered the fort's evacuation. That night, as the last of the Confederate
defenders stole away, Montgomery's brigade, the 54th included, formed
in reserve in anticipation of Gillmore's planned assault. Sunrise on the
seventh brought rumors that the rebels had abandoned Wagner, however,
and pickets soon confirmed those reports. Swails and his weary companions breathed sighs of relief, and Federal troops quickly occupied Fort
Wagner along with neighboring Fort Gregg, which the rebels had also
evacuated. "Up and down through the trenches and the parallels rolled
repeated cheers and shouts of victory," Emilio recalled. "It was a joyous
time; our men threw up their hats, dancing in their gladness. Officers
shook hands enthusiastically. Wagner was ours at last."

The fall of Wagner and Gregg elevated the 54th Massachusetts's reputation still more. The engineer Major Brooks effused that "in no military
operations of the war have Negro troops done so large a proportion and
so hazardous fatigue duty, as in siege operations on this island." General
Gillmore joined the chorus of praise, informing the troops that Forts
Wagner and Gregg had been "wrested from the enemy by your persevering courage and skill, and the graves of your fallen comrades rescued
from desecration and contumely."

Even though the men of the 54th Massachusetts had proven their mettle
as soldiers, Swails and his compatriots received constant reminders that
their color denied them the same respect and treatment their own supe-

riors accorded to their white countrymen. They could not help noticing, for example, that Black soldiers performed a disproportionate amount of the army's manual labor while their white counterparts remained idle in camp. "I must say that while the agreement and harmony amongst the white and black privates are almost perfect," Captain Charles Bowditch of the 55th Massachusetts wrote to his father, "yet among the officers of white regiments the officers of the blacks are looked down upon."

Especially disturbing were reports of racial rioting in New York City from June 13 through June 16, coincidentally when the 54th fought its first engagement at Sol Legare. Outraged by the imposition of a draft, protestors—mainly poor working-class men and Irish immigrants—took to the streets of New York, focusing their venom against wealthy citizens who could buy their way out of the draft for $300 and against African Americans, whom they viewed as responsible for the war and, when freed, as potential competitors for their jobs. Protestors looted and set fire to Black citizens' homes, burned Black boarding schools, destroyed the Colored Children's Orphanage that housed more than 200 children, lynched eleven Black men, and assaulted numerous others.

Swails and his fellow African American soldiers felt profound distress. "The startling news of the mobs, riots, incendiarism, pillage and slaughter, recently so rife in the North, particularly in New York City, has reached here," wrote Stephens from the 54th Massachusetts's encampment. "You may judge what our thoughts and feelings were as we read bulletin after bulletin depicting to the life the scenes of violence and bloodshed . . . simply for belonging to another race or class of people." Atrocities committed against New York's African Americans, he maintained, exceeded the French Revolution's excesses. "And even while your mob-fiends upheld the assassin knife, and brandished the incendiary torch over the heads of our wives and children and to burn their homes, we were doing our utmost to sustain the honor of our country's flag, to perpetuate, if possible, those civil, social, and political liberties, they, who so malignantly hate us, have so fully enjoyed," Stephens bitterly noted.

While the men of the 54th Massachusetts decried brutal racism on the home front, they received a jarring reminder of their second-rate status from the very government that had retained their services. When they mustered into the army in early spring, Governor Andrew had promised them the same pay as white soldiers, which for privates was thirteen dollars per month. The Black troops had received no pay since then, however, and assembled anxiously when the paymaster arrived at Morris Island to address them on August 5. The government was ready to pay them ten dollars a month, not thirteen dollars, the paymaster announced, and also planned to deduct three dollars for clothing, which would leave them only seven dollars a month. Deeply offended, the men unanimously refused to accept less than the promised thirteen dollars. When the paymaster cautioned that they might not receive any pay until Congress reconvened, their spokesmen replied that they had already waited five months and would wait even longer, if necessary. "Too many of our comrades' bones lie bleaching near the walls of Fort Wagner to subtract even one cent from our hard-earned pay," Corporal James Gooding wrote. "If the nation can ill afford to pay us, we are men and will do our duty while we are here without a murmur, as we have done always, before and since that day we were offered to sell our manhood for ten dollars a month." Standing on principle, the regiment's white officers refused to accept any pay until the Black soldiers received theirs. On September 27—almost two months later—the paymaster returned and repeated that he was still offering each of the regiment's soldiers seven dollars a month (after the clothing deduction). Everyone declined the offer and did so again when he repeated it three days later.

Colonel Montgomery, now commanding the 54th's brigade, expressed anger over the men's refusal of pay. Addressing the regiment, he launched into a tirade. "The paymaster is here to pay you," he announced, admonishing the Black soldiers that they "should not expect to be placed on the same footing with white men." Anyone who heard them shouting and singing, he railed, "can see how grotesquely ignorant you are." He reminded Swails and the rest of the regiment that he was the first officer in the country to employ "nigger soldiers," whom he had brought on as teamsters—"a nigger and a mule go very well together." He then made threats, telling the men that "in refusing to take the pay offered you, and what you are only legally entitled to, you are guilty of insubordination and mutiny, and can be tried and shot by court-martial." In closing, Montgomery resorted to insult. "A few years ago your fathers worshipped snakes and crocodiles in Africa," he declared. "Your features partake of a beastly character. Your features can be improved. Your beauty cannot recommend you. Your yellow faces are evidence of rascality. You should get rid of this bad blood. My advice to you is the lightest of you must marry the blackest women."

Montgomery's speech hit the dumbstruck soldiers like a thunderclap, or more aptly, like a dagger to the heart. Here was their commander, who held their lives in his hands, expressing the very attitudes and beliefs they had devoted their lives to ending. He thought they were no better than animals and should be grateful for whatever crumbs their white masters doled out to them. According to Stephens, Montgomery's spiteful remarks "fell with crushing outcome on the regiment." So deep was their anger that Swails and his fellow Black soldiers refused to acknowledge the colonel when he later visited their camp. "Grateful for the privilege to fight?" Stephens wrote a friend after Montgomery's diatribe. "For what are we to be grateful? Here the white man has grown rich on our unpaid labor—he sold our children—insulted our wives—shut us out from the light of education, and even kept the Bible from us. I think it a question of repentance on his part instead of gratitude on ours." Corporal Gooding was moved to write directly to President Lincoln. Noting that the Black troops had performed as expected, he asked, "Why can't we have a soldiers pay? The regiment do pray that they be assured their services will be fairly appreciated by paying them as American soldiers, not as menial hirelings. Black men, you may well know, are poor: three dollars per month for a year will supply their needy wives and little ones with fuel." There is no record that he received a reply.

The dispute over pay continued into the next year. Governor Andrew suggested that Massachusetts make up the difference, but the soldiers declined on the grounds that accepting his offer would present them "to the world as holding out for money and not from principle." It was the Federal government's obligation, they insisted, to treat them as the equals of white soldiers.

Swails stepped forward as a prominent spokesman for the right of Black soldiers to receive equal pay. Concerned that his family in New York was impoverished, he wrote the army's adjutant general in January 1864, "Since [April 1863] I have performed the duty of a soldier, and have fulfilled my part in the contract with the Government. But the Government having failed to fulfill its part of the agreement, in as much as it refuses me the pay and allowances of a Sergeant in the Regular Army, I therefore, hereby respectfully demand to be mustered out of the service of the United States." The adjutant general apparently failed to respond, but Swails remained in the ranks. Two months later, another officer in the 54th implored the authorities to "think of what the men do and suffer; think of the starving families. There is Sergeant Swails, a man who has fairly won promotion on the field of battle. While he was doing the work of the government in the field, his wife and children were placed in the poorhouse."*

In March 1864, after the 54th had suffered more casualties in a brutal engagement in Florida and still had received no pay, Private Edward D. Washington expressed the regiment's disgust. "Now it seems strange to me that we do not receive the same pay and rations as the white soldiers," he wrote in a letter home. "Do we not fill the same ranks? Do we not cover the same space of ground? Do we not take up the same length of ground in a graveyard that others do?" Black soldiers, he concluded, "have to go through the same hurling of musketry, and the same belching of cannonading as white soldiers do."

Finally, in June 1864, Congress authorized a regular soldier's wage for the Black troops. It was not until September of that year, however, that the promised funds were distributed to Swails and the men of the 54th Massachusetts.

During the months following the assault on Fort Wagner, Swails and his fellow soldiers remained deeply concerned about the fate of their captured compatriots. The Confederates had taken at least sixty of the regiment's men, some twenty of whom were wounded. General Beauregard, who knew that the African American troops had been imprisoned, directed that all wounded Federals be cared for regardless of their color. Confederate authorities, however, separated uninjured prisoners by color, holding white captives in warehouses and Black prisoners in the Charleston city jail and in Castle Pinckney, a fortress in the harbor. As

---

*Apparently, the representations about Mrs. Swails's dire situation were overblown, though perhaps not by much. According to one newspaper report, by the spring of 1864, she had "moved from her residence in Cooperstown, New York, to her mother's home in Elmira. She relocated based upon the recommendation of dear friends, who feared that her financial situation would lead her to placement in the pauper's pen." *Weekly Afro-American*, May 7, 1864.

for the Black prisoners' fate, Southern jurisprudence was clear. The law did not recognize an entity known as a Black soldier. African Americans fighting against the Confederacy were either free Blacks inciting rebellion, in which case the penalty was death, or were slaves in rebellion, thus deserving of either death or a return to slavery. They were not eligible, as white soldiers were, to participate in prisoner-of-war exchanges. A gallows erected in the yard of the Charleston jail convinced the prisoners that the Confederates intended to hang them. Soon they were bound over to local courts for trial.

On July 30, President Lincoln threw down the gauntlet, declaring that "the law of nations and the usages and customs of war, as carried on by civilized powers, permit no distinction as to color in the treatment of prisoners of war." Hence, to "sell or enslave any captured person on account of his color, and for no offense against the laws of war, is a relapse into barbarism and a crime against the civilization of the age." If the Confederates insisted on their barbaric practices with respect to captured Black soldiers, the president proposed to respond in kind. "It is therefore ordered that for every soldier of the United States killed in violation of the laws of war, a Rebel soldier shall be executed, and for every one enslaved by the enemy or sold into slavery, a Rebel soldier shall be placed at hard labor on public works, and continue at such labor until the other shall be released and receive the treatment due a prisoner of war."

The *Charleston Mercury* denounced Lincoln's pronouncement as an abomination, insisting that the "uncivilized use" of Blacks as soldiers could not be condoned. Four Black soldiers captured at Wagner were former slaves, and South Carolina governor Milledge Bonham sided with public opinion and ordered them to stand trial. On September 8, the litigation began in the Charleston Police Court, where attorney Nelson Mitchell represented the prisoners. He did so skillfully, persuading the judge that, despite their color, they were legitimate soldiers, protected by the rules of war, and that the court lacked jurisdiction to try them as rebellious slaves. Visiting the jail at midnight, Mitchell called out to his clients, "All of you can now rejoice. You are recognized as United States soldiers." The Black captives remained in prison in Charleston until December 1864, when Confederate authorities transferred them to a prisoner-of-war camp in Florence, South Carolina.

Gillmore's occupation of Morris Island and capture of Forts Wagner and Gregg significantly advanced the Union goal of taking Charleston. For the next several months, the general and his naval counterpart, Rear Admiral Dahlgren, focused on capturing Fort Sumter, which controlled access to Charleston Harbor. Although Union firepower relentlessly pounded the citadel, its defenders held on, stalemating Gillmore and Dahlgren's efforts. For the men of the 54th Massachusetts, those months meant more digging and hard labor, often under artillery fire.

Good news, however, arrived for Swails. In November, he received word that he had been promoted to acting sergeant major of the 54th Massachusetts—the regiment's highest noncommissioned rank and, consequently, the highest rank available to a Black soldier.

Anxious to achieve meaningful victories in his Department of the South, Gillmore turned his attention to Florida. Until now, the Sunshine State had been a backwater in the conflict. It held virtually no strategic importance, and its manpower pool was shallow. Its beef and crops, however, helped provision Confederate armies fighting elsewhere, leading Gillmore to conclude that opening an offensive in Florida might advance several important Union objectives. "First, to procure an outlet for cotton, lumber, timber, turpentine, and the other products of the state," he advised his superiors. "Second, to cut off one of the enemy's sources of commissary supplies. . . . Third, to obtain troops for my colored regiments. Fourth, to inaugurate measures for the speedy restoration of Florida to her allegiance, in accordance with instructions which I have received from the President by the hands of Maj. John Hay, assistant adjutant general." This last justification—taking steps calculated to help bring Florida back into the Union—referenced a request from President Lincoln for Gillmore to assist Major Hay in procuring signatures on loyalty oaths in Florida, which were necessary to secure the state's readmission. In light of the upcoming presidential election in November 1864, Lincoln had a political stake in Florida's restoration to the Union, as the state's electoral votes under a reconstructed government were likely to be in his favor.

Gillmore appointed Brigadier General Seymour to head this Florida expedition. Based on his background, Seymour seemed a good choice, although his costly offensive against Fort Wagner raised serious questions. Recently recovered from his wounds suffered during that venture, he drew his expeditionary force from the units besieging Charleston, including Montgomery's brigade with the 54th Massachusetts. They were to travel to Jacksonville by ship and march west along the Florida, Atlantic, and Gulf Coast Railway, destroying trestles over the Suwannee River and other waterways.

In preparation for the movement, at 3:00 A.M. on January 29, 1864, Swails and the rest of the 54th Massachusetts left Morris Island on steamers bound for Hilton Head. "No more fatigue at the front!" Swails and his companions shouted as the island that had been their home for the past five months disappeared from view. "We'll have a rest from the sound of the guns!" That evening, Swails and the rest of the regiment camped on Hilton Head near the Pope plantation. "All enjoyed the change of landscape," Captain Emilio recalled, "green fields, trees, and herbage in place of the sand and sea wastes of Morris Island." Over the next few days, more regiments arrived at Hilton Head, including the 8th USCT, which joined Montgomery's brigade.

Late on February 5, the 54th Massachusetts received orders to march, and the men once again crowded onto steamers. Edward Hallowell had recently recovered from a wound received while assaulting Wagner and returned on October 27, 1863, now promoted to colonel and once again in command of the regiment. In the dark of night, Hallowell, along with Company F and Acting Sergeant Major Swails, boarded the *General Hunter*—the very transport that had taken them across Folly River to Morris Island for the assault against Wagner—and headed for Jacksonville. Their next adventure awaited them.

CHAPTER FIVE

I Now Recommend His Being Allowed to Serve as a Commissioned Officer

The seven thousand troops assigned to Seymour's Florida expedition steamed south on twenty-eight transports, aiming to rendezvous at the mouth of the Saint Johns River. They reached their destination near noon on February 7 and started toward Jacksonville, some twenty-five miles upriver. Toward evening, the town, which had suffered through three Union occupations and was in ruins, came into view. Women and children gathered on the riverbank, waving handkerchiefs at the approaching armada. When a few stray Confederate cavalrymen fired at the 54th Massachusetts as the soldiers disembarked, Seymour directed the regiment's Appleton, who was now a major, to "take his men and catch the rebels." Appleton's troops spread along the city's streets and drove off the Confederates, capturing a few of them. Colonel Hallowell then marched the entire 54th to Jacksonville's western edge, where Swails and the regiment bivouacked for the night.

The next day, Seymour started west along the railroad. Scouting ahead was a mounted "Light Brigade," as the general called it, commanded by Colonel Guy V. Henry, followed by three infantry brigades under Colonels William Barton, Joseph Hawley, and Montgomery. The 54th Massachusetts was to remain behind in Jacksonville, with Colonel Hallowell serving as the city's military commandant.

Colonel Henry pushed rapidly westward the night of February 8, bypassing a Confederate encampment at Camp Finegan and capturing a rebel outpost and five artillery pieces at Ten Mile Run. Early the next morning, he occupied Baldwin, some twenty miles west of Jacksonville. "In general appearance, a person would not take it for a town in the North," a

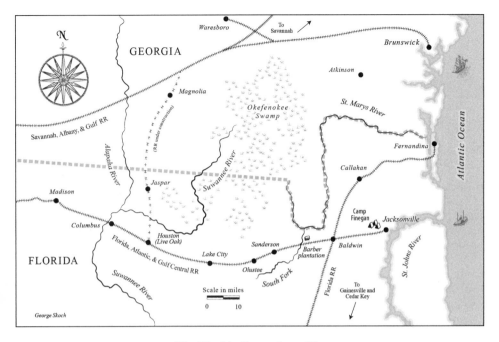

The Florida Campaign, 1864

Black soldier later wrote, "nor even disgrace the name of the town by applying it." Sparse as it might be, Baldwin was a critical railroad junction, where
the Jacksonville–Tallahassee line crossed a set of tracks that originated
north of Jacksonville at Fernandina and continued southwest through
Gainesville to Cedar Key on the Gulf of Mexico. Henry's men raided local
warehouses and confiscated camp equipment, cotton, rice, molasses, blankets, flour, sugar, and other items that Seymour later valued at $500,000.

The next morning, the Light Brigade continued west along the tracks,
scooping up provisions until they reached Moses Barber's plantation on
the south fork of the Saint Marys River. They skirmished briefly with a
Confederate outpost at a ford, then pressed on to Sanderson, where they
encamped. Not one to wait, Henry set out at 2:00 the next morning and
ventured west until encountering Confederates near Lake City. Uncertain of the rebel contingent's strength and concerned that he might be
too far advanced for Seymour to assist, the colonel retired to Sanderson
to await the other brigades' arrival.

Generals Gillmore and Seymour, meanwhile, heatedly debated whether the expeditionary force should continue west or hunker down and consolidate its hold on Jacksonville. Gillmore favored occupying Lake City and perhaps venturing on to the Suwannee River to destroy the railroad bridge there. Seymour, however, insisted that neither objective was advisable, arguing that Union sentiment in the region was negligible, transportation difficulties plagued the operation as it was, and Confederate forces were gathering in unknown strength. The wise decision, he insisted, required falling back to Jacksonville. One of Seymour's officers concluded that "neither general had much faith in the success of the expedition and that it was purely a political move, intending to drive the rebels to the west side of the Suwannee River . . . and thus enabling the larger part of the state to have a vote in the coming presidential election." Deferring to his subordinate, Gillmore directed Seymour to concentrate at Baldwin "without delay" and to fortify Jacksonville's environs.

On February 15, Gillmore left Florida for Hilton Head, instructing Seymour in no uncertain terms against advancing into Florida's interior without his permission. Seymour proceeded to ignore this order, writing Gillmore two days later that he had changed his mind and renewed his westward push with his entire force, including the elements still in Jacksonville, aiming to destroy the railroad bridge over the Suwannee. "By the time you receive this I shall be in motion," he informed the department commander. Astounded by this insubordination, Gillmore dispatched an aide with written instructions directing the wayward general to suspend his forward movement and return to Baldwin. Unfortunately, the officer failed to reach Seymour before the ill-fated venture had begun. Hay, President Lincoln's secretary now busy collecting signatures on loyalty oaths in anticipation of Florida's readmission to the Union, noted that Seymour had been acting "very unsteady and queer" and described the general's latest about-face as but another of his "violent alternations of timidity and rashness, now declaring Florida loyalty was all bosh, now lauding it as the purest article extant, now insisting that Beauregard was in front with the whole Confederacy and now asserting that he could whip all the rebels in Florida with a good brigade."

Unknown to Seymour, Brigadier General Joseph Finegan, an Irish immigrant and veteran of several of the war's major battles, was amassing a formidable Confederate force to thwart the Union advance. Finegan initially lacked sufficient troops to engage the Federals and could only try to slow the enemy's progress. Hoping to accomplish more, he requested reinforcements from Beauregard, who sent him Brigadier General Colquitt's and Colonel George Harrison's brigades. By February 19, Finegan had some 5,200 soldiers at his disposal. He deployed this force near Olustee Station across Seymour's likely route, the strong defensive line anchored to the left on Ocean Pond, a huge inland lake that prevented any flanking attack from the north, and to the right on a large cypress swamp.

The expeditionary force started west along the railroad early on February 20. Riding in front, Henry's cavalry encountered Finegan's lead elements near Sanderson and drove them back toward Olustee Station. Advancing part of his force to intercept the Federals, Finegan waged an aggressive defense. Seymour, on the other hand, committed his army piecemeal, much as he had done when attacking Fort Wagner, and frittered away his numerical advantage. After several hours of combat and having suffered heavy casualties, the Union general ordered a retreat.

Part of the 54th Massachusetts—Companies C, D, F, and K, including Acting Sergeant Major Swails—had left Jacksonville on February 12 and settled in at Baldwin. On the eighteenth, when Seymour decided to continue west, the remainder of the 54th reunited with the regiment's elements at Baldwin and marched to the Barber plantation, where Seymour had encamped. The next morning, as the general advanced to his ill-fated encounter with Finegan near Olustee Station, the 54th prepared to follow as a rear guard, leaving two companies at Barber. Stepping off in conjunction with the 1st North Carolina—another Black regiment that had been folded into Montgomery's brigade—Swails and his companions sang, "We're bound for Tallahassee in the morning." The roadway paralleled the railroad, and the marching troops enjoyed crisp air warmed by glints of sunlight filtering through the tall pines lining their path. By the time the 54th reached Seymour, the battle was well advanced. Musketry and cannon fire rumbled in the distance, prompting one of Swails's fellow soldiers to remark, "That's home-made thunder." Responded another, "I don't mind the thunder if the lightning don't strike me!"

Suddenly, an orderly appeared and called out for the regiment's commander. Colonel Hallowell sprang to his feet, spoke hurriedly with the orderly, and directed the 54th to start for the front at the double-quick. Marching at full tilt, the soldiers cast aside their knapsacks and blankets to lighten their load. Nearing the front, they met a flood of wounded men and stragglers streaming back. The fleeing Federals called out, "We're badly whipped," and "You'll all get killed." Still the 54th pressed on, encouraged by Sergeant Garnet G. Cezar, who shouted their new battle cry, "Three cheers for Massachusetts and seven dollars a month!"

Seymour informed Colonel Hallowell that "the day was lost" unless the 54th held the enemy in check while the general formed a new defensive line in the rear. When word arrived that Confederates were deploying off the Federal left flank, Hallowell directed the regiment into a forest south of the road, then climbed onto a stump to better view the action. Confederate musketry and artillery raked the 54th's position, but the troops, including Swails, refused to budge. The regimental band played "The Star-Spangled Banner" as soldiers belted out the lyrics at the top of their lungs. "Its thrilling notes, soaring above the battle's gales, aroused to new life and renewed energy into the panting, routed troops," recalled a man in one of the retreating outfits.

Company D, where Swails was now assigned, shifted to better fend off an expected rebel assault. The acting sergeant major reported the change in position to Hallowell and started back to his outfit when a spent bullet struck his right temple, seriously wounding him. Seeking medical aid, he fell exhausted on the roadway, too weak to call for help. A passing lieutenant, however, recognized Swails and flagged down a cart, which took him to the medical station at Sanderson.

The 54th Massachusetts hunkered down in the woods amid a brutal firefight, holding on until it became the last remaining Union outfit on the field. As the sun dipped to the horizon, the soldiers of the 54th gave nine hearty cheers to make it appear they were receiving reinforcements, then marched off the field with their backs to the Confederates. Of the regiment's approximately 530 soldiers who went into battle, 13 were killed, 8 were missing, and 66 were wounded, one of whom was Swails. As at Fort Wagner, Seymour's offensive had failed, but the 54th Massachusetts had performed heroically. The general had asked Hallowell to "go in and save the corps," and the colonel's men had done precisely that. As one of the regiment's soldiers put it, they had "checked the enemy, held the field, and were the last to leave—and covered the retreat."

One reason that Swails and his fellow African American soldiers fought so doggedly was their fear that, if captured, the Confederates would either murder them or sell them into slavery. Their concerns were well founded. Shortly after the battle, a rebel cavalryman heard musketry crackling and asked what was happening. "Shooting niggers," an officer replied. "I have tried to make the boys desist but I can't control them." An injured white soldier looked on in horror as a Southern officer approached a wounded Black man and shot his brains out. In response to a flag of truce and an inquiry about Black prisoners and their officers, Confederate authorities responded, "We will hang every damned negro officer we catch." A Bay State soldier later wrote that he would "never forget the cry of 'Kill the God damn sons of bitches' when the 54th Massachusetts Volunteers went into the fight." In his opinion, "we are compelled to take this in our own hands. The Johnny Reb will find out the niggers won't die so fast."

Contempt appears to have been mutual, as reflected in a Black soldier's letter a few months later. White Floridians, he explained, "do not seem to understand anything but that they are the most God-foresaken looking animals on earth." In his opinion, "they look *mean;* they live *meanly,* act *meanly,* and they don't *mean* to be anything but *mean;* and it is safe to assert that they are very *mean.* To think that these fellows voted Florida out of the Union without the aid of the primitive inhabitants—alligators—is simply preposterous."

The 54th's retreat through Sanderson was disheartening. "The narrow road was choked with a flowing torrent of soldiers on foot," recalled Captain Emilio. "In this throng generous and self-sacrificing men were seen helping along disabled comrades, and some shaking forms with bandaged heads or limbs, still carrying their trusty muskets. About the sides of the road exhausted or bleeding men were lying, unable to proceed, resigned, or thoughtless of inevitable captivity." Forming part of the covering column, Hallowell's soldiers reached the Barber plantation at 2:00 A.M. and collapsed from exhaustion. Seven hours later, they set off again, marching four miles past Baldwin when they received orders to turn around and retrieve a broken-down train filled with wounded soldiers. "It was a hard trial for the footsore and hungry men to retrace their steps," Emilio later wrote, "but the thought of the cars laden with wounded nerved them to the task, so they faced about cheerfully." Many of the wounded, of course, were Black, and the men of the 54th were not about to abandon them to the Confederates. Marching back, they attached ropes to the train cars and hauled them several miles to Camp Finegan, where horses waited to take over. The regiment, wrote a Sanitary Commission doctor who witnessed the spectacle, "did what ought to insure it higher praise than to hold the field in the face of a victorious foe—with ropes it seized the engine (now useless) and dragged it with its doomed freight for many miles. They knew their fate if captured; their humanity triumphed," he proclaimed. "Does history record a nobler deed?"

After a brief rest at Camp Finegan, the 54th trudged on to Jacksonville and bivouacked on its former campground, having marched over 120 miles, fought a battle, and hauled a locomotive during the previous week. Among the wounded men transported to Jacksonville was Acting Sergeant Major Swails.

Seymour had lost the Battle of Olustee, and his soldiers were not shy about criticizing his generalship. "We have had a fight, a licking, and a footrace," an officer in the 54th wrote to a friend in Boston. "There seems to have been a strange ignorance of the number, position, and plans of the rebels," the 54th's Sergeant Stephens complained. "There is not a shadow of a doubt that the enemy knew our numbers and purposes perfectly well, and calmly awaited our approach, and whipped us completely. And how can they help frustrating any movement we may undertake," he asked, "if so much criminal leniency is extended to them?" The African American troops "behaved creditably—the Fifty-fourth Massachusetts and First North Carolina like veterans," Seymour wrote in his battle report. "It was not in their conduct that can be found the chief cause of failure, but in the unanticipated yielding of a white regiment [the 7th New Hampshire] from which there was every reason to expect noble service, and at a moment when everything depended on its firmness."

"There is much feeling about it all here," Colonel Higginson wrote home from Beaufort, "and Gen Gillmore is freely censored. He threw it all, last night, on Gen Seymour who, he said, had disobeyed orders. But the whole plan of the Expedition of course is Gen G's responsibility."

The Confederate bullet that struck Swails's head did no lasting damage. According to his pension records, Swails received treatment in Jacksonville, then transferred to Beaufort, where he received additional care at the general hospital. Despite his wound, his star was quickly rising. Swails had distinguished himself during the assault on Fort Wagner and in the siege that culminated in its capitulation. He had also excelled in performing his duties as acting sergeant major, so much so that Colonel Hallowell, in his official report on the Florida expedition's offensive at Olustee, singled him out for commendation. "Sergeant Stephen A. Swails, acting sergeant-major," he effused, "deserves special praise for his coolness, bravery, and efficiency during the action; he received a severe but not mortal wound in the head."

Governor Andrew, who had demonstrated boldness in the spring of 1863 by raising the 54th Massachusetts in the first place, decided the occasion had arrived to take another bold step. Based on Hallowell's recommendation, on March 11 he formally appointed Swails second lieutenant, a commissioned officer in the US Army. At this juncture, the War Department had approved commissions for only a few African American surgeons and chaplains who neither commanded troops nor engaged in combat. Never before had an African American soldier in a combat role received this honor. The governor did not explain why he selected Swails as his test case for this revolutionary step, but Andrew's reasoning likely included the sergeant's impeccable military record, bravery in battle, intelligent and eloquent demeanor, and perhaps most importantly, complexion—the fact that to observers who did not know him, he appeared white. While Andrew candidly observed that Swails was "darker than most officers," as Captain Emilio noted, "to all appearances he was a white man."

The *Weekly Anglo-African,* a prominent Black newspaper, proudly announced Swails's appointment. "The first commission to a colored officer has just been issued to 2d Lt. Swailes [*sic*] of Western New York," the newspaper stated. "We may now at length take rank among civilized nations." A soldier from the 54th Massachusetts wrote to the newspaper that he "looked forward to the day when any colored man, who is competent, shall be assigned to the position that his qualifications call him to. We have sergeants in this Regiment that can handle a company as well as any white man in the army," he continued. "Will any of them be promoted to a captaincy? We shall see."

An important step remained, however, before Swails's appointment could become formal; the War Department had to discharge him as an enlisted soldier and officially muster him as an officer. The implications of such a move were momentous. Commissioning Swails as a line officer not only rendered him eligible for advancement up the chain of command but also opened the possibility that he might exercise authority beyond the company and regimental level, that he—a Black man—might occupy a position exercising authority over white soldiers. The latter possibility violated deeply ingrained racial taboos. It was widely believed that Blacks were innately inferior to whites and lacked the intelligence and reasoning ability to hold positions of authority. The idea of a Black officer giving orders to white soldiers was anathema.

Swails was on leave in Elmira recovering from his head wound until mid-May, but when he rejoined his regiment, Colonel Hallowell made a routine request for approval to Major General John G. Foster, who had replaced Gillmore as the Department of the South's commander. When Foster failed to act promptly on the request, Hallowell asked Governor Andrew to intervene on Swails's behalf. Foster finally checked with Washington authorities and reported that they had denied him permission to discharge Swails. A War Department memorandum candidly explained that the reason for denial was Swails's "color, he being partially of African blood." According to the document, the secretary of war, "whose personal attention was called to the case," believed that "it was contrary to public policy to receive persons of African descent into the service as Commissioned Officer[s]."

Hallowell refused to take no for an answer, but found himself in a ticklish situation. Committed to the cause of Black equality, he felt outrage that the authorities were denying Swails promotion solely because of his race. The colonel decided to permit Swails to wear the uniform of a US Army officer and to discharge the duties of his rank—only, however, when he was with the 54th Massachusetts. In mid-September, Hallowell expressed his frustration to Governor Andrew. "Sergeant Stephen A. Swails is not yet mustered as an officer because he is believed to have African blood in him! How can we hope for success to our arms or God's blessing in any shape while we as a nation are so blind to justice?"

In the meantime, word spread that Swails now dressed and acted like a commissioned officer. In October, the 127th New York's Captain Richard Allison wrote headquarters, "Stephen Swails (Colored) is acting as Second Lieutenant in the 54th Regiment Massachusetts Volunteers, although he is not mustered in as an officer. This is in strict violation of General Order No. 74." Headquarters forwarded the letter to Hallowell and requested an explanation. The colonel responded by scrawling in the letter's margin that Swails had been "commissioned as a 2nd Lieutenant, and has been acting as such since May 12, 1864, awaiting muster. He has only been on duty as an officer over his own men, and with the members of this regiment. He acts as 'regimental Officer of the Day' and as Officer of the Guard, but has never been put on duty when he would come in contact with officers or men of other units. I believe it would be prejudicial to the service to compel him to resume his chevrons."

Swails also pitched in, writing Foster to "respectfully ask a Discharge from the service (as an enlisted man), by reason of promotion, for the purpose of being mustered in on my commission." The efforts were still in vain. On October 18, Foster ordered that "1st Sergeant Stephen A. Swails is hereby relieved from duty as 2nd Lieutenant, and will in future wear the uniform of a 1st Sergeant."

Undeterred, Swails paid Foster a visit. Hallowell's and Andrew's advocacy, combined with Swails's personal appeal, partially won the general over, and Foster approved a furlough for Swails to press his case with the War Department. Anxious to set the record straight, Foster wrote Andrew that it was the Washington authorities who had "decided that [Swails] could not be mustered in as an officer, owing to his being of African descent." The general went on to note that Swails "has, on several occasions, distinguished himself in battle, and was severely wounded at Olustee. All the officers of his regiment have the highest respect for him and are anxious to have him made an officer of their regiment. I have given Sergeant Swails a furlough, and write this in testimony of his good conduct, and assure you that in refusing to discharge him as an enlisted man, I have acted under particular orders from the War Department." The governor forwarded the general's letter to the war secretary, adding that while Swails was not "of white Caucasian blood, [he was] a man of character, and intelligence, a soldier of superior merit, a gentleman and worthy the recognition of gentlemen." In closing, he urged that "Mr. Swails, having fairly earned promotion and having the capacity and talent to command men, ought not to be delayed in his muster in as a 2nd Lieutenant."

Swails went on leave on November 12, visiting his family in Elmira and apparently also the War Department in Washington to personally press his case. His persistence and the advocacy of Andrew, Hallowell, and other officers brought Foster around. "Sergeant Swails is so nearly white that it would be difficult to discover any trace of his African blood," the general assured Washington authorities. "He is so intelligent and of such good character that after a fair trial I now recommend his being allowed to serve as a commissioned officer." This time the War Department relented and authorized Foster "to discharge Sergeant S. A. Swails, 54th Massachusetts Volunteers (colored) and to muster him into service as Second Lieutenant."

On February 8, 1865, Swails formally mustered in as a second lieutenant. Captain Emilio later remarked, "This decision, persistently solicited and finally granted, must rank high with the moral victories wrung from the general government by the regiment and its founders." The dam had burst, and additional Black officers were mustered in later that year. One of the newly commissioned Black officers in the 55th Massachusetts observed that there was "much feeling in the Regiment among the officers against these promotions of colored men in respect with white officers, but all the best officers are in favor of it."

Swails had returned to the 54th Massachusetts in mid-May 1864 after recovering from his head wound. During his absence, the regiment had seen little action, engaging primarily in guard and patrol duties. It left Jacksonville on April 17 and started down the Saint Johns River on transports, headed back to South Carolina. "The day of departure was delightful," Captain Emilio wrote. "Those few weeks in the 'land of flowers' left recollections never to be effaced of soft skies, beautiful plants, perfume of orange and magnolia, the resinous odor of the pines; of battle and defeat, severe marches, midnight alarms, and long hours of picket in woody solitude."

The next morning, the ships carrying the 54th pulled into Stono Inlet and headed into Folly River. Disembarking onto familiar ground, the troops marched across Folly Island in a heavy rainstorm, traversed Lighthouse Inlet, and camped once again on the sands of Morris Island. Union forces still occupied the island, although hostile artillery fire sporadically rained in from Fort Sumter and other rebel fortifications. The place felt a lot less crowded, however, as many outfits that had participated in the offensive against Fort Wagner had left for other fields. Colonel Hallowell briefly took command of the post, but Colonel Montgomery soon replaced him. "Our daily duties of fatigue and grand guard went on unvaryingly week after week," Emilio reported.

Toward the end of June, the tempo changed. Hoping to break the deadlock in front of Charleston, the Union high command launched a multipronged offensive to threaten the city and stretch the beleaguered rebel line until it broke. The plan called for Brigadier General William Birney, recently arrived with a fresh brigade of Black soldiers, to advance up the Edisto River and sever the Charleston–Savannah rail line at Adams Run. At the same time, Brigadier General John P. Hatch would take two brigades to Seabrook Island, cross to John's Island, and threaten to cross the Stono River at Rantowle's Bridge and attack the city from that angle. Simultaneously, Brigadier General Alexander Schimmelfennig's force, including the 54th Massachusetts, planned to advance onto James Island and confront the Confederates there. Topping everything off would be a naval bombardment from the Stono.

The coordinated Union elements began deploying late on July 1, 1864. At 6:30 P.M., Swails and the rest of the 54th Massachusetts crossed to Folly Island, marched to the Stono River, and proceeded by steamer to Cole's Island. Setting out shortly before daybreak the following morning, they retraced in reverse their route from Sol Legare Island of the year before. The road and bridges had been repaired, prompting Emilio to remark that "there was little to remind us of the old pathway." On reaching James Island, the 54th repelled the rebels opposing them and settled down in waist-high marsh grass near the line they had held the previous year. The day grew hotter and "became almost unbearable to the skirmishers, stifled in the high grass on the line, who were compelled to maintain a prostrate and immovable position," an officer recounted. The men suffered terribly until they received orders shortly before midnight to camp in a nearby cornfield. When headquarters discovered a company had failed to return, Swails set off with ten men to bring it in, which he did without incident. Mosquitoes became so persistent that General Schimmelfennig smeared his face with kerosene, "choosing to endure the odor rather than the loss of blood."

Key to the movement on James Island was an amphibious assault on Fort Johnson. When that attack failed on July 3, Union headquarters decided to cancel the entire operation. The 54th remained stationary, along with several other units, until nightfall on the ninth, when it received orders to withdraw. Threading their way back to Morris Island, Swails and his fellow soldiers settled into camp, welcoming the opportunity to rest, bathe in the surf, and don clean clothes.

The 54th Massachusetts passed the rest of the summer and fall in routine garrison duty on Morris Island. A break came in early September, when some 560 captured Confederate officers arrived on the island and were confined in a prison camp next to Fort Wagner—now renamed Fort Strong—fully exposed to Confederate fire from Sumter. This prisoner transfer culminated a brutal tit-for-tat between the opposing sides. Reports in the South condemning inhumane conditions in Northern prisoners spurred a retaliatory response from Union authorities, which gained steam when Congress's Committee on the Conduct of the War published a pamphlet in May 1864 documenting purported intentional mistreatment of Union soldiers in Southern prison camps. The pamphlet spurred War Secretary Stanton to reduce rations afforded Confederate prisoners of war to a quarter of the recommended amount and to otherwise exacerbate their hardships. The US Sanitary Commission then published a report condemning what it termed a "premeditated plan, originating somewhere in the rebel counsels, for destroying or disabling the soldiers of their enemy." The Confederate Congress responded with its own report, denying any intentional mistreatment of Union prisoners and blaming prison overcrowding on the North's decision to terminate prisoner exchanges. The war of words culminated in late summer, when Federal authorities removed 600 prisoners from the Northern prison camp at Fort Delaware, Maryland, and sent them to encampments in Union-held areas of the South, including Morris Island, where they served as "human shields" against the Confederate artillery bombarding the island.

The 54th Massachusetts was assigned to guard the prisoners, and one can assume the irony of placing Black soldiers to guard Confederates officers was not lost on anyone. Captain Emilio noted that the captives included "tall, lank mountaineers, some typical Southerners of the books—dark, long-haired, and fierce of aspect,—and a lesser number of city men of jauntier appearance." Scarcely any two dressed alike, sporting an assortment of straw and slouch hats and forage caps, cavalry boots and ragged shoes, and tattered uniforms and overalls. "They made a poor showing for chosen leaders of the enemy," thought Emilio. "It did seem that men of their evident mental and intellectual caliber—with some exceptions—might be supporters of any cause, however wild or hopeless." Although the situation seemed ripe for conflict, guards and prisoners tried to get along, leading one officer of the 54th to remark that many of the stockade's inmates appreciated "such attentions and politeness as could be extended within the scope of our regulations." When guards apprehended five Confederate officers naked and trying to swim away, the 54th's lieutenant colonel brought them into his tent, offered them "stimulants," told them he did not blame them and even invited them to try to escape again if they wished, and then returned them to the stockade.

Toward the end of November, Swails went on furlough. When he returned to his regiment in January 1865, the Civil War's end was near. General Robert E. Lee's surrender at Appomattox was only four months away, but for 2nd Lieutenant Swails, they would be eventful months.

Robert Gould Shaw.
Collection of the Massachusetts Historical Society.

Edward Needles Hallowell.
Collection of the Massachusetts Historical Society.

The 54th Massachusetts assaults Fort Wagner. This 1867 engraving was made by an unknown artist based on the painting by Thomas Nast.
Author's collection.

In the Trenches before Wagner.
From *Harper's Weekly*, August 29, 1863, p. 553.

SIXTY-FIVE MEMBERS OF THE SOUTH CAROLINA LEGISLATURE, 1868-1872

[From a photograph in possession of the Editor]

Twenty-two of the entire legislature of 155 members could read and write; several could write only their names; 41 signed by an X mark. Of the 98 negro members, one paid $83 taxes, 30 together paid $60, and 67 paid none. Of the 57 whites, 11 Conservatives paid $194; 22 Radicals paid $297; and 24 Radicals paid none. None of the state officers, except the lieutenant governor, paid taxes. The taxes levied amounted to $2,000,000 a year, and in addition the bonded debt was increased by about $20,000,000 by 1872. When the legislature and state officers went out of office they paid taxes on a great deal of property.

Sixty-Five Members of the South Carolina Legislature, 1868–1872.
This photographic collage depicts the Republican members of the first South Carolina legislature during Reconstruction. Swails is identified in the key as the figure on the far left, bottom row.
Courtesy Schomburg Center for Research in Black Culture, Jean Blackwell Hutson Research and Reference Division, New York Public Library.

South Carolina governors Robert K. Scott, Franklin J. Moses,
Daniel Chamberlain, and Wade Hampton.
Courtesy South Carolina Department of Archives and History.

Veterans of the three Black regiments from Massachusetts—the 54th Infantry, 55th Infantry, and 5th Cavalry—parade before the Shaw Memorial in Boston in 1897. William Carney carries the flag; Swails is in the group behind him. *Collection of the Massachusetts Historical Society.*

Portrait of Stephen A. Swails, by Michael Del Priore, commissioned
June 4, 2008, for permanent display in the South Carolina Senate chamber.
Courtesy Billy Jenkinson.

CHAPTER SIX

Crowned with Laurels

On November 11, shortly before Stephen Swails embarked on his second furlough, General Foster received instructions to cooperate with Major General William T. Sherman, who was preparing to leave Atlanta and initiate his "March to the Sea." To assist in this venture, Sherman wanted him to "break the Charleston and Savannah Railroad about Pocotaligo about the 1st of December." Foster accordingly gathered some 5,000 troops at Port Royal for this purpose, including eight companies of the 54th Massachusetts.

Headed by Brigadier General Hatch, the soldiers left Hilton Head the night of November 28 and steamed up Broad River toward Boyd's Landing in the stream's headwaters. Heavy fog and unfamiliarity with the inland river system delayed their progress. The troops disembarked at the landing the evening of November 29, but several units then took the wrong road—"it is said that the guide employed was either ignorant or faithless," an officer in the 54th reported—delaying the advance another day. The Confederates were now fully alerted to Hatch's approach and entrenched along a slight rise known as Honey Hill. Starting forward early on November 30, the Federals soon encountered the enemy line. In a battle that lasted all day, Hatch failed to make headway against the strongly posted rebels and sustained about 750 casualties. "The generalship displayed was not equal to the soldierly qualities of the troops engaged," a participant wrote in explaining Hatch's defeat. "There appears to have been a lack of foresight in the preparations."

Over the next two months, the 54th Massachusetts participated in several minor military actions assisting Sherman's march toward the coast. Savannah fell on December 21. Toward the last week of January 1865, Sherman's army advanced into South Carolina, some elements coordinating with Hatch. Swails returned from furlough during these operations and rejoined the 54th Massachusetts.

As Confederate resistance collapsed, Hatch's troops marched toward Charleston, crossing marshes and rice plantations adjoining the Combahee, Ashepoo, and Edisto Rivers. Field hands greeted them "with joyful demonstrations," and refugees poured into their camps. Rain pounded down in torrents, but the exhausted soldiers slogged on toward Charleston. "We are all destitute of clothes, and some have not as much as a shoe upon their feet," Sergeant John Collins of the regiment later wrote, "but when you look at the suffering condition of the poor slaves, we can stand all: only give us our liberty and freedom, and we will give our lives for liberty, for we love that well-known sound."

Finally, on February 19, word reached Hatch that Charleston had surrendered. "Cheer after cheer rang out; bonfires were lighted; and the soldiers yelled long and frantically," Emilio recalled. "Far into the night nothing else was talked about around the camp-fires." Union troops from Morris Island, it developed, had already occupied the city, including two of the 54th Massachusetts's companies that had remained behind. Crossing to Charleston on rowboats, they had marched through town to The Citadel, a military academy near the city's northern boundary. "Being the first considerable body of colored soldiers to arrive," a man in the 54th reported, "their march through the streets was a continual welcome from crowds of their people of both sexes."

Shortly after noon on February 23, Hatch's little army, including Swails and the 54th Massachusetts's main body, reached the Ashley River. "There, across the river, we saw Charleston, long the mecca of our hopes," an officer wrote. Confederates had burned the bridge across the Ashley, so Swails and his companions camped by the river, waiting several days for transports to take them across. Early on February 27, the steamer *Croton* ferried them over, and the Black northeasterners marched into the war-ravaged city. Freed slaves poured into the streets to greet them. "On the day we entered that rebellious city," Sergeant Collins recollected, "the streets were thronged with women and children of all sizes, colors, and grades—the young, the old, the halt, the maimed, and the blind. I saw an old colored woman with a crutch, for she could not walk without one, having served all her life in bondage—who, on seeing us, got so happy that she threw down her crutch and shouted that the year of jubilee had come." Marching up Meeting Street through the center of town, the 54th Massachusetts entered Magnolia Cemetery and camped among the tombstones.

Charleston was in shambles. Looting was rampant, fires blazed everywhere, and explosions at abandoned Confederate ordnance depots shook the city. "I hear on all sides very discouraging accounts of the state of affairs in Charleston," Gillmore informed Hatch. "That no restraint is put upon the soldiers; that they pilfer and rob houses at pleasure; that large quantities of valuable furniture, pictures, statuary, mirrors, etc., have mysteriously disappeared—no one knows wither or by what agency; and that matters are generally at sixes and sevens." The record is silent concerning whether any soldiers from the 54th Massachusetts participated in the looting, although they were permitted to visit the city. The men were especially interested in the jail, where their friends captured during the Morris Island operations had been imprisoned. Black and white captives were housed separately, but one African American had managed to slip a note to a white soldier who was being released on parole. It read, in part, "the privations of the white soldiers are nothing in comparison to ours and in our destitute condition, being as it were without friends, and in the enemy's hands, with an almost hopelessness of being released, and not having heard from our families and friends since we were captured." The jail was now empty, its captives now held in the prisoner-of-war camp at Florence, South Carolina.

Less than two weeks after entering Charleston, Swails and the 54th Massachusetts boarded a steamer bound for Savannah, where they settled into a camp formerly occupied by Sherman's soldiers. After the devastation in Charleston, Savannah was a welcome sight. Swails strolled along the town's shaded streets, enjoying its numerous parks and elegant residences. The spring weather was refreshing, gardens were in bloom, and the soldiers filled their days with picket duties. It seemed to Swails and his companions that the war must soon end in light of Sherman's march through Georgia and South Carolina, Major General Philip Sheridan's victory in the Shenandoah Valley, and Grant's grinding siege of Lee's Confederates at Petersburg. They expected that their fighting days were over, that they would soon be returning home.

New orders arrived on March 25 that dashed their expectations. The

54th Massachusetts was to report to Georgetown, South Carolina, to participate in a raid deep into Confederate territory.

The raid was Sherman's brainchild. The Confederates had parked several locomotives and considerable rolling stock on two railroads between Florence and Sumter, South Carolina, and had stockpiled vast military stores in the same area. Sherman considered the trains and supplies "important" and requested their destruction "at once." He left the details to Brigadier General Edward E. Potter, who would be leading the expedition, volunteering only that "2,500 men lightly equipped with pack mules only, could reach the road either from Georgetown or the Santee Bridge." Potter could draw his force, Sherman suggested, from the Union troops occupying Charleston and Savannah. It was critical, he stressed, that the "cars and locomotives should be destroyed, if to do it costs you 500 men." Speed was of the essence. "Let it be done at once," Sherman insisted, "and select your own point of departure."

Formerly a lawyer in New York, Potter had served in North Carolina and later with General Foster during the operations around Charleston. Georgetown, a port city some fifty miles north of Charleston that Potter had helped capture in late February, provided a perfect location for launching the raid. The 54th Massachusetts reached that town on March 31, with the rest of the troops arriving over the next two days. The "Provisional Division," as the expeditionary force was called, contained two brigades, one under Colonel Phillip P. Brown Jr. and the other under Colonel Hallowell, the latter consisting of the 54th Massachusetts and companies from other all-Black regiments, which led to Hallowell's outfit being nicknamed the "Colored Brigade." Altogether, the Provisional Division contained slightly more than the suggested 2,500 soldiers.

Inclement weather delayed Potter's departure, but he was underway by April 5, heading well into the interior of South Carolina. "The country we passed through is the most desolate imaginable," Lieutenant Edward L. Stevens of the 54th scrawled in his diary. "We passed but two or three houses all day and those of the meanest kind." Conditions improved as Swails and the Provisional Division pressed inland, foraging for supplies and burning any cotton and mills that they encountered. Multitudes of slaves seeking to escape bondage joined the column,

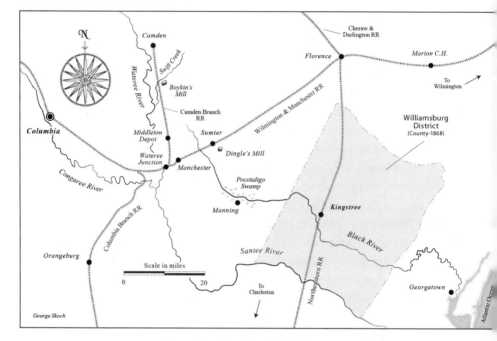

Potter's Raid in South Carolina, 1865

including children. "Little boys and girls of such tender ages, as at home would not be trusted outside the yards . . . , keep up with us marching twenty miles a day," Stevens wrote. "It is sad and yet encouraging to see the hope on their countenances and their perfect trust in us."

Potter's initial objective—the town of Kingstree, which would later play a pivotal role in Lieutenant Swails's life—proved difficult to reach, as Confederates had dismantled the bridge over the Black River. Sliding northeast, the raiders hit the Northeastern Railroad, tore up several miles of track, and destroyed the railroad bridge across the Black. By evening on April 8, Hallowell's troops had reached Manning, where they helped construct a bridge over Pocotaligo Swamp. From there they advanced toward Sumter. "We must have burned over half a million dollars worth of cotton today," Stevens thought, estimating that 1,000–1,500 escaped slaves had abandoned their plantations and were tagging along with the Union force. According to Captain Emilio, the 54th Massachusetts dispatched details that destroyed three locomotives, fifteen cars, and Manning's fully equipped railroad machine shop.

On April 9, following a spirited skirmish at Dingle's Mill, Potter's outfit reached Sumter. After setting fire to many of the town's buildings, the troops started looting businesses and homes, singing "John Brown's Body" and "Year of Jubilee." A brave lady was tending to her flower garden when soldiers appeared in her yard, apparently intent on mischief. Mounting her porch, she shouted, "I'll shoot the first man who puts his foot on that step," and clicked her sheers behind her back. Her ruse worked, and the intruders fled. The next day, the Provisional Division, according to Potter's report, "destroyed all the railway buildings and machine shops, 4 locomotives, and 20 cars," and "the railway track was torn up and trestle-work burned for six miles on either side." He later added that his men also destroyed the freight depot, storehouses, offices and employee quarters, and a million feet of lumber.

The Provisional Division departed Sumter on April 11 and headed toward Manchester, followed by most of the town's Black population. According to a major in one of Potter's white regiments, "The negroes had flocked to us by the thousands and in all sizes and colors," trailing the army in "a most absurd procession, and lengthening for miles on the road." On reaching Manchester, the 54th Massachusetts continued five miles farther to Wateree Junction, on the Wilmington and Manchester Railroad. A nighttime reconnaissance revealed that the junction held a rich collection of water tanks, locomotives, and railroad cars. One locomotive had its steam up, and the soldiers hurried to capture it before it escaped. Lieutenant Swails, Sergeant Frank Welch, and eighteen picked men rushed across a trestle and into the junction, Swails pounding hard in front. On reaching the locomotive, the lieutenant leaped into the engine cab and waved his hat in triumph. Surprised, the rebel engineer jumped from the train and ran for his life while the train hands fled down the railroad embankment and into an adjacent swamp.

A Union sharpshooter posted near the junction mistook Swails for the train's engineer and fired at him, hitting him in his right arm. While the lieutenant nursed his wound, a former slave alerted the Federals that more trains were on the other side of the Wateree River. Crossing on a trestle, Captain Charles E. Tucker and his company found three locomotives and thirty-five cars, which they disabled. Upon returning, they discovered other men from the regiment, apparently ignorant of their expedition, had set the trestle on fire. Anxious not to become separated from the rest of the force, the captain led his soldiers through smoke and flame across the span. "Scarcely had we accomplished the passage," Tucker wrote, "when it tottered and fell, a heap of blazing ruins."

The Federals decided to take the undamaged engines and cars at the junction back to Manchester. After they had loaded injured soldiers onto the trains, they started off. Lieutenant Swails, his bloody arm now in a sling, took charge of the lead locomotive and drove slowly down the tracks. Soon, however, the engine failed, forcing him to abandon his locomotive, which the troops burned along with other discarded railway debris.

The Provisional Division remained in the Manchester area for several days, including April 14, which marked four years since the first shots of the war at Fort Sumter. Lieutenant Stevens saw it as an occasion for celebration. "The great, great emancipation of hundreds of thousands of slaves," he wrote in his diary, "the advance of freedom and liberal ideas, our success in arms are very encouraging and lead us to hope for speedy peace." Former slaves poured into Union camps in such numbers that Potter finally dispatched the 32nd USCT to escort them to the Santee River, where they would board boats for Georgetown. On the evening of the seventeenth, Potter's division marched into Camden, its band playing "John Brown's Body." The Confederates, the general soon discovered, had moved their rolling stock to Boykin's Mill, eight miles away.

The next day, while keeping some troops in Camden to destroy the railroad, Potter took the rest of his force to Boykin's Mill. The Confederates stoutly defended their position on the far side of Swift Creek, thwarting attempts by the Federals to cross. In a brave charge along the crest of a dam, the 54th Massachusetts ended the deadlock and punched through the rebel line. "The heroes of Wagner and Olustee did not shrink from the trial, but actually charged in single file," wrote Joseph T. Wilson of Company C. "The first to step upon the fatal path went down like grass before the scythe, but over their prostrate bodies came their comrades, until the enemy, panic-stricken by such determined daring, abandoned their position and fled."

The action at Boykin's Mill was the 54th Massachusetts's last battle, arguably the Civil War's last engagement of consequence. Lee had surrendered the Army of Northern Virginia on April 9, and General Joseph E.

Johnston, commanding the Confederate army opposing Sherman, had entered into surrender negotiations the day before the battle at Boykin's Mill. The 54th's Lieutenant Stevens had the dubious honor of being the last officer killed in the war. During the fighting at Boykin's Mill, Stevens, riding conspicuously on his white horse, made an inviting target for the Confederates. "Do you think you can stop him?" Confederate colonel Artimus Darby Goodwyn inquired of his fifteen-year-old courier, Burwell H. Boykin. The young man replied affirmatively by shooting Stevens in the head, killing him.

After Boykin's Mill, Potter's troops started back toward Georgetown. Reaching Middleton Depot on April 20, they struck a goldmine: two miles of railroad crammed with abandoned locomotives and train cars packed with Confederate ordnance, quartermaster's stores, and railway machinery. Potter's men filled the cars with gunpowder and shells and ignited them, destroying eighteen locomotives and 176 railroad cars. "The explosion was terrific, and for several hours it seemed as if a battle was being fought," an officer recalled. Swails and the rest of Potter's force marched into Georgetown late on April 25, having been on the road for twenty-one days and covering nearly three hundred miles. In all, the general reported that his Provisional Division had destroyed thirty-two locomotives, 250 cars, many miles of track, 5,000 bales of cotton, and otherwise severely disrupted Confederate supplies. Most importantly, it had secured the freedom of some 6,000 slaves.

Orders soon arrived for the 54th to return to Charleston, which it did during the first week of May. Colonel Hallowell assumed command of the city's defensive perimeter, and the 54th took up quarters in The Citadel, each morning holding a ceremony on the square fronting the military academy. "The men were allowed frequent passes outside the spacious Citadel grounds," Captain Emilio wrote, "making friends with the colored people, which in some cases resulted in a partnership for life."

Perhaps in writing those words, Emilio had Lieutenant Swails in mind. Quite likely on one of his forays from The Citadel, Swails met Susan Aspinall, a twenty-two-year-old mulatto. Her father, Albert Aspinall, was a tailor and one of the few free African Americans of modest wealth in Charleston. According to city records, he owned real estate valued at $1,500. The records also show that on April 18, 1866, Swails and Miss Aspinall were married by an Episcopal minister at the Aspinall family home in Charleston.

But what about Stephen Swails's wife Sarah, who had borne him two children—Stephen Jr. and Minnie—and in 1865 was living in Elmira with his brother, Jesse? The record is silent concerning whether Stephen and Sarah were actually married or when, if ever, she learned about his marriage to Susan. We do know, thanks to the historian Hugh MacDougall's thorough examination of census records, that she later married a Mr. Jackson, who died before 1880, and that she was living in 1910 in Brooklyn with her daughter, Minnie. Whether she ever spoke again with Swails, we simply do not know.

In later years, Susan Aspinall certified in pension documents that "she had no knowledge of the said Stephen A. Swails, ever having married prior to his marriage with [her]" and that he "represented himself as a single, unmarried man" whom she, "during her whole married life, had no reason or cause to believe otherwise."

Meanwhile, Swails continued his rise in the military. On June 8, 1865, Governor Andrew promoted him to first lieutenant, and on July 1, an order declared, "First Lieutenant Swails is hereby detailed as Acting Adjutant, 54th Massachusetts Volunteers, and will be obeyed and respected accordingly."

Preparations moved apace for the regiment's discharge from service. On August 14, the 54th was relieved from garrison duty and camped in Mount Pleasant, across the Cooper River from Charleston. Hallowell made his headquarters at the home of Elias Whilden, a planter and former mayor of the town, whose five sons had fought for the Confederacy. One of those sons, John Marshall Whilden, had been captain of The Citadel cadets who fired on the *Star of the West* on January 9, 1861, precipitating the Civil War. The 54th Massachusetts was discharged on August 20, then traveled to Boston Harbor and camped on Gallop's Island. They received their final pay and formal discharge papers on September 1.

The next day, the regiment ferried to Boston's Commercial Wharf and marched to the statehouse, where Governor Andrew addressed them. "Everywhere along the route cheers went up from admirers, and friends rushed to shake hands with relatives or acquaintances among the officers and men," Emilio recounted. "Through the throng of citizens lining the curb, the fifty-fourth marched, welcomed at every step, with the swing only acquired by long service in the field, and the bearing of seasoned soldiers."*

The *Boston Evening Transcript* captured the mood of the celebration. "The Fifty-fourth Massachusetts Regiment, the pioneer State colored regiment in this country, recruited at a time when great prejudices existed against enlisting any but so-called white men in the army, when a colored soldiery was considered in the light of an experiment almost certain to fail, this command—which now returns crowned with laurels, and after two hundred thousand of their brethren, from one end of the traitorous South to the other, have fought themselves into public esteem—had such a reception today as befitted an organization the history of which is admitted to form so conspicuous a part of the annals of the country."

It is likely that Swails attended the regiment's final discharge in Boston in early September. Later that month, he returned to South Carolina and Susan Aspinall—a passenger list for the ship *Alhambria* published on September 20, 1865, shows one S. A. Swails traveling from New York to Charleston. A new career in politics, more dangerous in many respects than his military service, awaited him.

---

*When Andrew's governorship ended in January 1866, he returned to the practice of law and remained active in politics. He died at home the following year from apoplexy.

CHAPTER SEVEN

This Is a White Man's Government

The end of the Civil War brought massive social dislocation to South Carolina and most of the South. The 1860 census had counted some 700,000 residents in the Palmetto State, of whom 400,000, or almost 60 percent, were Black slaves. Virtually the entire enslaved population lived in poverty, a situation that freedom did little to alleviate. The newly liberated Blacks were generally unemployed, illiterate, and without property, many of them lacking the skills and knowledge necessary to navigate their new world.

White citizens' racial prejudices and fears further complicated defining the appropriate role for Black freedmen in Southern society. Slavery had touched every aspect of South Carolina's social, political, and economic life, and that experience shaped white attitudes toward the recently liberated African Americans. As a prominent South Carolina minister remarked, slavery had "fashioned our modes of life, and determined all of our habits of thought and feeling, and moulded the very type of our civilization."

For decades, Southern preachers, politicians, and community leaders had embraced white supremacy and warned of the dangers of emancipation. South Carolina's Reverend James Furman, for example, had insisted that the Holy Scriptures sanctioned slavery and stressed that if the slaves were freed, "every Negro in South Carolina and every other Southern state will be his own master; nay, more than that, will be the equal of every one of you. If you are tame enough to submit, abolition preachers will be at hand to consummate the marriage of your daughters to black husbands." Another prominent South Carolina minister professed that "some of the most eminent of the Old Testament saints were slaveholders" and cited Paul's return of an escaped slave to his master as biblical authority for the Fugitive Slave Act, which required the return of runaways.

During the 1850s, proslavery arguments from the pulpit turned especially strident. Churchgoers heard that slavery was "the most blessed and beautiful form of social government known; the only one that solves the problem, how rich and poor may dwell together; a beneficent patriarchate." The *Central Presbyterian* affirmed that slavery was "a relation essential to the existence of civilized society." By 1860, Southern preachers felt comfortable advising their parishioners that "both Christianity and Slavery are from heaven; both are blessings to humanity; both are to be perpetuated to the end of time."

Southern politicians espoused a similar theme, inquiring who could "without indignation and horror contemplate the triumph of negro equality, and see his own sons and daughters in the not distant future associating with free negroes upon terms of political and social equality?" Abolition, they warned, would surely mean "the two races would be continually pressing together," and "amalgamation or the extermination of the one or the other would be inevitable." The end of slavery, they predicted, would either "plunge the South into a race war or so stain the blood of the white race that it would be contaminated for all time." Could Southern men "submit to such degradation and ruin," they asked, and responded with the admonition, "God forbid that they should."

In a typical presentation, a prominent politician warned that if slaves were freed, "the black race will be in a large majority, and then we will have black governors, black legislatures, black juries, black everything. Is it to be supposed that the white race will stand for that? It is not a supposable case." He predicted that "war will break out everywhere like hidden fire from the earth. We will be overpowered and our men will be compelled to wander like vagabonds all over the earth, and as for our women, the horrors of their state we cannot contemplate in imagination. We will be completely exterminated," he declared, "and the land will be left in the possession of the blacks, and then it will go back to a wilderness and become another Africa or Saint Domingo."

In the fall of 1860, John Townsend, owner of a cotton plantation on Edisto Island, South Carolina, warned that abolition meant "the turning loose upon society, without the salutary restraints to which they are now accustomed, more than four millions of a very poor and ignorant population, to ramble in idleness over the country until their wants should drive most of them, first to petty thefts, and afterwards to the bolder crimes of robbery and murder." The planter and his family were then "not only to be reduced to poverty and want, by the robbery of his property, but to complete the refinement of the indignity, they [were] to be degraded to the level of an inferior race, be jostled by them in their paths, and intruded upon, and insulted over by rude and vulgar upstarts. Who can describe the loathsomeness of such an intercourse;—the *constrained intercourse* between refinement reduced to poverty, and swaggering vulgarity suddenly elevated to a position which it is not prepared for?"

Nonslaveholders, Townsend predicted, also faced dangers. "It will be to the non-slaveholder, equally with the largest slaveholder, the obliteration of *caste* and the deprivation of important privileges," he cautioned. "The color of the white man is now, in the South, a title of nobility in his relations as to the negro," he reminded his readers.

In the Southern slaveholding States, where menial and degrading offices are turned over to be performed exclusively by the Negro slave, the status and *color of the black race* becomes the badge of inferiority, and the poorest non-slaveholder may rejoice with the richest of his brethren of the white race, in the distinction of his color. He may be poor, it is true; but there is no point upon which he is so justly proud and sensitive as his privilege of caste; and there is nothing which he would resent with more fierce indignation than the attempt of the Abolitionist to emancipate the slaves and elevate the Negros to an equality with himself and his family.

Now the slaves were free, and Southern whites feared the predicted horrors were imminent. For decades, preachers, politicians, and community leaders had bombarded them with one apocalyptic vision after another—emancipation, race war, miscegenation. The challenge now was to find a strategy for holding the barbarians, for whom Swails was soon to become a prominent spokesman, at bay.

Late in 1861, Union inroads along the South Carolina, Georgia, and northern Florida coasts freed thousands of slaves, inspiring Treasury Secretary Salmon P. Chase, a fervent abolitionist, to authorize the "Sea Island Experiment," designed to help newly liberated African Americans in their transition to freedom. Under this program, freed slaves, supervised by Treasury Department officials, were hired to work on their former plantations for forty cents a day and rations, while private organizations in partnership with the government established schools and provided teachers throughout the Sea Islands. In mid-1862, the War Department assumed responsibility for the program, and Brigadier General Saxton became the new director. A native of Massachusetts, the thirty-eight-year-old West Point graduate had served in several of the war's theaters and presented a striking figure with his "black hair and luxurious English whiskers." Saxton maintained the existing system but added a layer of military officers and partitioned the territory under Union control into districts and subdistricts.

After occupying Savannah in December 1864, General Sherman, following Secretary of War Stanton's instructions, issued Special Field Orders 15, reserving for the settlement of freedmen an area extending thirty miles inland from Charleston south to Jacksonville. Saxton, who was tasked with implementing Special Field Orders 15, issued "possessory titles" granting each freedman's family forty acres but held off letting them occupy their plots, except on Edisto Island, until he received further authorization and direction from the government.

In March 1865, Congress formalized the program by creating within the War Department the Bureau of Refugees, Freedmen, and Abandoned Lands, known popularly as the Freedmen's Bureau. The bureau sought to advance the "general well-being" of freedmen and white refugees by providing food, fuel, clothing, health care, and education; to make available, for rent or for sale, land and housing; to assist in obtaining employment; and to resolve disputes relating to labor contracts, back pay, pensions, and domestic affairs, including the legalization of marriages. Major General Oliver Otis Howard, the bureau's commissioner, not surprisingly selected Saxton as assistant commissioner to administer the bureau's program in South Carolina.

Saxton's assignment proved daunting. "Many of the farms and plantations had suffered from devastation, neglect, and abandonment," a historian of the Freedmen's Bureau observed; "tools, implements, and seed were scarce; hundreds of war-weary landowners were returning without money or means to face the bleakness of the times; and thousands of freedmen had become physically displaced and emotionally disoriented during the conflict and its aftermath." Complicating matters even more, the bureau quickly became a political football. Congress failed to fund the enterprise, assuming that its cotton farms would provide sufficient profit, but the Treasury Department appropriated the farms' proceeds over Saxton's objection. Then Andrew Johnson, who became president following Lincoln's assassination in April 1865, issued a proclamation restoring property rights to former rebels who took the oath of allegiance and set in motion a process for the former rebellious states to return to the Union. By year's end, of the 800,000 acres once controlled by the Freedmen's Bureau, only about 75,000 acres remained.

President Johnson's proclamation and the rebellious states' return to the Union severely hampered Saxton's ability to implement the bureau's objectives. He balked at returning appropriated Sea Island plantations to their former white owners, a stance that ultimately cost him his job. In January 1866, General Howard relieved him as South Carolina's assistant commissioner and replaced him with Brigadier General Robert K. Scott, an Ohio doctor who had commanded a regiment and a brigade during Sherman's campaign through Georgia and the Carolinas. One of Scott's first duties was to return properties occupied by freedmen on Edisto Island to their prewar owners.*

The Freedmen's Bureau faced outright hostility from South Carolina's white population. Southerners viewed it as an alien institution imposed on them by the hated Northerners. According to John William DeForest, a New Englander in the bureau's Greenville office, "To my native infamy as a Yankee I added the turpitude of being a United States military officer and the misdemeanor of being a sub-assistant commissioner of the Freedmen's Bureau." The *Charleston Mercury* denounced the organization as "an army of malignant Southern haters, negro fanatics, and needy adventurers, backed in their power by the army of the United States." The bureau's goal, the newspaper declared, was to "Africanize the South, and to put the white man under the negro." Saxton later advised Commissioner Howard that "the late rebels hate and slander us." The

---

*Saxton remained with the military until he retired from active duty in 1888. He died on February 23, 1908, at his home in Washington, DC.

South's white population was "profoundly impressed with the belief," he warned, "that a black man has no rights which a white man is bound to respect" and saw in the bureau "a great stumbling block in the way of their schemes to overthrow the policy of the government and make the freedman a slave in everything but name."

Suspicion of the bureau extended to the highest reaches of South Carolina's government. As the Civil War sputtered to a close, President Johnson appointed Benjamin Franklin Perry the state's provisional governor. A lawyer, newspaper editor, and politician, Perry was a native-born South Carolinian and an outspoken Unionist. He was, however, no friend of the Black man, and his attitudes toward race reflected those of his fellow white Southerners. "The African has been, in all ages, a savage or a slave," he announced. "God created him inferior to the white man in form, color, and intellect, and no legislation or culture can make him his equal. His color is black, his head covered with wool instead of hair, his form and features will not compare with the Caucasian race, and it is in vain to think of elevating him to the dignity of the white man." Above all, Perry advocated the proposition that Blacks must not vote or otherwise participate in the political process. "This is a white man's government," he insisted, "intended for white men only."*

Governor Perry's actions matched his words. He reinstated former Confederate officials and reaffirmed state laws passed during the war years. Shortly after becoming governor, he scheduled a provisional state constitutional convention, which his appointment required him to do, to amend the state constitution. Only residents who had taken an oath of allegiance to the United States and had been otherwise qualified to vote in December 1860—the date of the ordinance of secession—could vote for delegates. Stated bluntly, African Americans could not vote. Not surprisingly, the delegates, who were all white, dutifully amended

---

*Perry's statement echoed a speech by Confederate vice president Alexander Stephens, who had proclaimed that the Confederacy's cornerstone rested on the "great truth that the negro is not equal to the white man; that slavery, subordination to the superior race, is his natural and normal condition." As many Southerners now saw it, the very danger that their politicians had warned them about before the war had come to pass, and the Freedmen's Bureau was the catastrophe's insidious agent. Dew, *Apostles of Disunion*, 14.

the constitution to abolish slavery and rescind the ordinance of secession but failed to grant former slaves the same rights, such as voting or holding public office, accorded to white citizens. "Many coats [worn by the convention's attendees] showed Confederate buttons," a newsman observed, a sartorial choice that he facetiously attributed to "the necessity of poverty rather than the choice of disloyalty, I judge."

The convention also called for the election of a governor and a new state legislature. James L. Orr, who had raised a Confederate regiment at the beginning of the Civil War, was elected governor, and the newly elected legislators, most of whom belonged to the prewar elite, proceeded to pass the Black Codes, a set of laws aimed at keeping former slaves in an inferior status. While the Black Codes did give the freedmen certain rights and recognized slave marriages, they expressly provided that African Americans "are not entitled to social or political equality with white persons" and included provisions forbidding Blacks from owning firearms or from working at occupations other than farmer or servant without paying an exorbitant fee. These laws also provided that "servants" who committed acts justifying their discharge could be brought by their "masters" before a magistrate, who was empowered to "inflict, or cause to be inflicted, on the servant, suitable corporal punishment, or impose upon him such pecuniary fine as may be thought fit, and immediately to remand him to his work."

In December 1865, Stephen Swails took a position with the Freedmen's Bureau and soon emerged as a significant force in South Carolina's contentious political vortex. Swails was no stranger to racial prejudice. The Columbia race riots had greeted him into the world as an infant, then he grew up in a society that offered him little opportunity for advancement and treated him with suspicion because of his race. He had faced discrimination in the army, which denied him the same pay accorded to white soldiers and resisted commissioning him as an officer because "African blood" coursed through his veins. Through persistence, he had surmounted the military's racial barriers. But as he soon learned, white Southerners' deeply ingrained racial hostility posed challenges of a much greater magnitude.

The Freedmen's Bureau first assigned Swails to a district that included the Sea Islands near Charleston, perhaps because he was familiar with the region from his service with the 54th Massachusetts. Little information about his activities there survives, although judging from the detailed narrative written by a bureau employee in Greenville, agents "bore varied responsibilities that would have taxed the combined capacities of a social service worker, an administrative official, a labor conciliator, and a judge." Their job required them to "supervise labor contracts between employers and freedmen, to administer rations and clothing to the destitute freedmen, to promote and supervise schools for the Negroes, to provide transportation where it would serve a beneficial purpose, to investigate complaints and disputes between the Negroes themselves or between Negroes and whites, to forestall any acts of violence against the Negroes, or any unfairness to them in the courts, to report such cases as could not be forestalled, and to maintain industry and good conduct among the Negroes themselves."

We do know that on one occasion, Swails accompanied two former plantation owners to Wadmalaw Island south of Charleston, where they hoped to recover appropriated property they had previously owned. The freedmen who now lived on the site were aghast that the former owners wanted to retrieve their plantations, as this was Sea Island land that had been included under Sherman's Special Field Orders 15. When the angry settlers surrounded the agent and his two white companions, Swails backed them off by drawing his pistol and showing them a letter of authorization from Saxton. Rather than take any risk, however, he and his party quickly left. A freedman who witnessed this display claimed that if Swails had not been present, the two white men might not have escaped alive.

On June 21, 1867, Swails became special duty agent in Kingstree, South Carolina. A small inland town seventy miles north of Charleston, Kingstree was a farming community and the seat of Williamsburg District. The district—after the 1868 Constitution, "county" replaced the term "district"—contained only about 15,000 residents, two-thirds of whom were former slaves. Families of modest means farmed the relatively flat terrain, which bore no comparison to the richer plantations of the state's coastal region. Swails had passed near Kingstree in April 1865 with Potter's Provisional Brigade during its raid.

After the war, the region's planters voiced concern that the liberated slaves would no longer work their fields. Their solution was to adopt a resolution agreeing to pay their former slaves a "living wage" if they remained. As the new Black citizens had no other practical options, most of them accepted the arrangement and stayed on as tenants. But when the labor contracts came up for renewal late in 1866, the landowners proposed lowering the "living wage" to six dollars a month, inspiring the freedmen to consider whether to demand higher pay or move to Florida or Texas, where free land and good jobs supposedly abounded. Rumors quickly spread that the former slaves had illegally raised six military companies and intended to take over the district. The farmers called upon the government to investigate, and Assistant Commissioner Scott of the bureau determined the freedmen were simply conducting peaceful protests against the white planters' requirement that they sign year-long work contracts for negligible pay. The *New York Times* concluded that "the whole thing originated from fear on the part of the planters that the freedmen would claim a proper remuneration for their labor."

The federal government had established a garrison in Kingstree immediately after the war, and relations between US officials and the local populace had become less than amicable. In one episode, a Treasury agent arrested a tavern keeper for selling cotton formerly owned by the Confederate government. The local sheriff, however, freed the man and arrested instead the Treasury agent, who the garrison's commandant promptly released. Tensions abated, however, during 1866, when the populace seemed content with the initial labor contracts, so the garrison closed. But toward year's end, following the freedmen's dissatisfaction with the lowered "living wage" and rumors of a violent Black takeover, the situation changed. White tempers flared when Commissioner Scott denounced rumors of imminent violence by the Black population as white farmers' fabrications to prevent freedmen from meeting to discuss the wage issue. After disaffected whites threatened to kill a US officer, Scott expressed concern that "the feelings of the [white] people about Kingstree were so antagonistic to the presence of a Bureau officer, that a number of evil-disposed people had threatened to take the life of such officer; consequently a garrison had to be established there, for the preservation of peace and good order." Reinstitution of the garrison and the increased US military presence exacerbated tensions still more.

Then on January 7, 1867, Kingstree's jail caught fire, and twenty-two Black inmates, including two women, burned to death. Most of them had been imprisoned for nonviolent crimes, such as stealing cows, hogs, or rice. The only prisoner the jailers rescued was Robert Flynn, the sole white inmate. The tragedy further escalated racial tensions in and about the town. Three of the jail's officials were indicted on murder charges; tried in mid-April 1867, a jury acquitted all three after deliberating no longer than an hour.

Swails stepped into this cauldron of racial discord and quickly distinguished himself as a strong and effective spokesman for the district's Black majority. Hundreds of letters from his Freemen's Bureau days survive and demonstrate his mastery of firmness and tact in resolving disputes, not only among his freedmen constituents but also, more importantly, between them and their white landlords and employers. For example, shortly after arriving in town, Swails informed a physician named Cunningham that a freedman tenant had complained "that you have driven him off the plantation without just cause" and instructed the doctor to come to his office two days hence with the freedman "for the purpose of making a proper settlement." He assured the doctor that if the two men could settle their differences, there would be no punitive measures. He closed, however, with a firm reminder that "in no case can a freedman be discharged until after a proper investigation at this office." On another occasion, Swails informed a plantation owner that a freedman reported "you have discharged him and driven him off your place with threats of shooting and also refuse to pay him for what labor he has done." He directed the landowner to bring to his office "all accounts which you have against him for the purpose of having a proper investigation and settlement." Swails wrote another landlord in a similar vein: "Clem Watson, an old freedman, makes a statement that you have driven him off from your plantation, together with his daughter." He reminded the landlord that "under existing orders, no person can drive a freedman or woman from his place without coming to the proper office and making a full settlement of all points between the parties. In respect to the old man, I think it would be nothing more than charity to let him continue staying on your place until he gets what little crop he has planted, but if it is impossible to do this, then you will have to bring the parties to the office and settle for what labor has been done."

Swails also worked to ensure that destitute freedmen received adequate housing and food. The bureau's records are replete with requisitions for food and bills of lading for delivering sustenance to impoverished families. Not long after taking up residence in Kingstree, for example, Swails advised a landowner to "send the heads of families on your place on Tuesday, August 20, 1867, and I will issue to them corn and bacon," adding, "send bags to take the corn in." A week later, he corresponded with a landlord who "had a woman on his plantation who by accident had lost both feet." The landlord offered to keep the woman on if the bureau would assist by providing her with food, which Swails agreed to do.

As an assistant commissioner, Swails took pains to memorialize in writing his land and labor settlements. One such contract instructed "the Planters to furnish the said freedmen with permissions, and in addition each hand $100.00 on or before first day of January, 1868." Swails also required that "for previous time he was at work, the Planters to pay him $5.00 per month for that time, in addition to the above $100.00." He assiduously followed up on breaches of these contracts. In September 1867, for example, he informed a landowner: "Sam Wilson (Freedman) makes a complaint that you are trying to defraud him out of the crop which he has made on the place worked by you. I deem it my duty to warn you that in case you continue in this you will bring trouble on yourself as you are evidently acting contrary to orders of the Asst. Comm. of this Bureau." The following month, he dealt firmly with a landowner who had failed to comply with his decision, instructing the offender to "give the parties the two-thirds as was agreed at this office on Monday, October 2, 1867. You will also understand that I am saying those parties have a perfect right to stay in the place until they have their full share of the crops. In case I hear of any more threats I shall consider it my duty to report the case to the military authorities. I have advised the parties to proceed to harvest their crops." In another letter, he warned a landlord: "You are wronging these people, and you will certainly get into trouble if you continue in this way. You will not be allowed to defraud these people in any way," he wrote, adding, "if you do not settle this matter, I will have to settle by military force." A more vigorous advocate for the district's freedmen is difficult to imagine.

Swails's attention to detail is evident from his written instructions. As an example, in October 1867 he enlisted the assistance of a Mr. William Walker, requesting him to "visit the plantation of Mr. Bennett Gordon and settle the differences between Mr. Gordon and the free people on his place. You will inform the parties that they must gather in the crop and store it in a safe manner until all is gathered. When all is gathered, you will divide the crop according to the agreement made. If there is some dispute between the parties in regards to the agreement, you will satisfy yourself as to what is the most fair and just. You will receive a percentage of the crop of both parties such as all will agree to."

By late 1867, many of Swails's cases were ending up in court, which led him to request permission to retain counsel for the freedmen. He was engulfed by "a great many troublesome cases," he informed his superiors, and believed "the people would be benefitted by having some lawyer to have to look after their interests." In a report summarizing his first months in Kingstree, Swails related that of the many complaints lodged in court against freedmen, he had determined that most "were frivolous . . . and thrown out for want of evidence." While "depredations" were still frequent, he was happy to state that "there have been no cases of shootings since I have been on duty." Most matters brought to his attention involved disputes over crops, "but they are generally frivolous and easily settled," he wrote. In conclusion, Swails assured his superiors that "there is a definite improvement in all things connected with the freedmen since last year although much still remains to be done."

In only a few months, Swails had established himself as the person Williamsburg District's freedmen could count on to effectively intercede on their behalf with the white power structure. He had also demonstrated to the district's white population that he was a fair and efficient arbiter. Swails knew everyone in the district, and everyone knew him. His performance in the Freedmen's Bureau post served as a compelling springboard into South Carolina's political maelstrom.

CHAPTER EIGHT

The Political Boss of Williamsburg County

Since the end of the war, white South Carolinians had firmly resisted allowing the state's Black majority to vote or otherwise participate in governmental affairs. Enraged by the provisional South Carolina General Assembly's passage of the Black Codes, the state's federal military commander, Major General Daniel Sickles, nullified the legislation and proclaimed that the state's laws had to apply equally to all citizens. In April 1866, Congress passed a Civil Rights Act that prohibited states from discriminating on the basis of color and, two months later, approved the text of the 14th Amendment, granting citizenship to all native-born Americans. The 14th Amendment was anathema to many white Southerners. "Give the negro political equality and he will legislate social equality," they warned. South Carolina's legislature refused to ratify the amendment, which only amplified the federal government's backlash. In March 1867, Congress passed the First Reconstruction Act, dividing the South into five military districts and requiring the inhabitants of each Southern state to live under martial law until they ratified the 14th Amendment and permitted all male citizens, regardless of race, to elect delegates to a new state constitutional convention, which was to draft a state constitution providing for universal male suffrage.

Also in March 1867, public meetings in Charleston, Beaufort, and Columbia led to the formation of South Carolina's Republican Party, composed primarily of freedmen and their white allies. The party's platform included universal suffrage and enforcement of the Reconstruction Act in the South. On October 16, the state's military commander scheduled an election for November 19 and 20, when the state's voters—who, under the Reconstruction Act, included Blacks—were to determine whether to hold a constitutional convention and to select delegates from their districts. White opposition was strong, and a convention of white citizens on November 6 issued an address denouncing Black suffrage because "as citizens of the United States we should not consent to live under negro supremacy nor should we acquiesce in negro equality." In sum, Black suffrage would result in "an ignorant and depraved race" being "placed in power and influence above the virtuous, the educated and refined." Since Southern Democrats, representing white interests, protested by boycotting the election, registered voters were predominantly Republican. In all, almost 80,000 Blacks signed up to vote, as opposed to some 46,000 whites. Because the election would be valid only if a majority of registered voters participated, many whites concluded that their best tactic was to stay home, thereby preventing the majority necessary to validate the election results.

Swails, who had moved to Kingstree in June of that year, threw his hat in the ring and ran as a Republican to represent Williamsburg District in the constitutional convention. "A Radical ticket was nominated for the Convention, to wit: Washington Darington (black), S. A. Swails (colored), and Olsten, plain," the *Kingstree Star* reported. "Of the competency of these individuals for Constitution-making we are not sufficiently acquainted with their history to speak, they all being of foreign importation; Swails from Massachusetts, Darington from Charleston, and Olsten from across the waters." District voters overwhelmingly approved the constitutional convention and selected Swails as a delegate. This election marked the first time in South Carolina's history that Black men had voted, and they came out in droves. Of the 124 delegates elected from across the state, 73, including Swails, were Black. The whites' "stay at home" tactic had failed miserably; only 2,211 whites had voted, as opposed to 68,876 Blacks, who constituted considerably more than a majority of the registered electorate.

The South Carolina Constitutional Convention met in Charleston on January 14, 1868. Swails played a prominent role, serving as chairman of the Rules and Regulations Committee and sitting on the Committee of Auditors. He took care, however, to avoid openly participating in the rancorous and confrontational debates favored by many participants and never delivered a speech, limiting his role to presenting reports, making procedural motions, engaging in private discussions, and lobbying other delegates. He voted generally with the Black majority, dissenting only over whether judges should be elected by popular vote instead of receiving their appointments from the legislature. According to a reporter who attended the convention, the seventeen Black delegates originally from the North played a leading role in deliberations. "They are the best debaters," he noted, and they displayed "a homely but strong grasp of common sense in what they say." He thought that the native South Carolinians were "not slow to acknowledge that their destinies really appear to be safer in the hands of these unlettered Ethiopians . . . than if confided to the more unscrupulous . . . white men in the body."

In early March, several of the convention's Black delegates paid a Saturday-night visit to one of Charleston's billiard salons. As they approached a table, the establishment's proprietor—a Mr. Fehrenbach—informed them that it was "against the rules of his room to permit them to play," and they left. The next day, Swails, accompanied by Brevet Colonel Moore and Colonel T. J. Robertson, both of whom were white, strode into the billiard salon, walked to a table, and began playing. As soon as he noticed Swails, Fehrenbach instructed him to leave. According to a newspaper account of the incident, "some high words passed," with Colonel Robertson reminding the proprietor that "this was a free republican government; that the negro was entitled to all the privileges of the white man; and that he would come with a party at 8 o'clock in the evening, and test the point as to whether his *friends* were entitled to play or not." Fearing trouble, Fehrenbach notified Charleston's police chief, who dispatched officers to the neighborhood.

As promised, at 8 o'clock sharp, Colonels Moore and Robertson returned with a party of delegates and began playing billiards. Swails then appeared, and one of the players stepped aside so he could join the game. As Swails picked up a cue, Fehrenbach announced that he was not permitted to play and asked him to leave. When Swails ignored this directive and continued playing, the salonkeeper summoned the police. "The civil officers had a long argumentative conversation with the military officer, who had his coat off and appeared determined to fight the matter through, but his better judgment advised discretion," the newspaper reported. Swails and his supporters left, according to the published account, "with the understanding that the opinion of both the military and civil government would be had on this question of privilege today."

Indeed, the next day—March 17, 1868—after fifty-three days of work, the convention presented its draft Proposed State Constitution to the voters for approval. The document, one of the most progressive of its time, began with an extensive declaration of rights modeled after the US Constitution but was even more inclusive, declaring that "all men are born free and equal—endowed by their Creator with certain inalienable rights, among which are the right of enjoying and defending their lives and liberties, of acquiring, possessing and protecting property, and of seeking and obtaining their safety and happiness." Nodding to the recent past, Article 1, section 5 provided that "this state shall ever remain a member of the American Union, and all attempts, from whatever source, or upon whatever pretext, to dissolve the said Union, shall be resisted with the whole power of the state." It went on to pronounce that "distinction on account of race or color, in any case whatever, shall be prohibited, and all classes of citizens shall enjoy equally all common, public, legal and political advantages."

Addressing an issue on everyone's mind, the draft constitution provided that "slavery shall never exist in this state" and forbade "involuntary servitude" except for convicted criminals. The document guaranteed all male citizens age twenty-one and above the right to vote "without distinction of race, color, or former condition," stipulating that the right to vote could not be denied because of "felony, or other crimes, committed while such person was a slave." Henceforth, representation in the state legislature would be according to population, rather than by population and wealth, as the former formula had required, with property qualifications for voting abolished. The new constitution envisioned a free public-school system, with twenty-four months of compulsory education for children between the ages of six and sixteen, adding that the "public schools, colleges and universities of this state supported in whole or in part by the public funds, shall be free and open to all the children and youths of the State, without regard to race and color."

Some delegates urged granting voting rights to women, but most viewed the measure as too extreme, so it failed. They did agree, however, to include a provision recognizing a wife's right to own property that could not be seized to satisfy her husband's debts and to make divorce legal for the first time in the state.

In April 1868, South Carolina held a referendum on the proposed constitution. The Democratic Party complained that the document raised the prospect of "negro rule and supremacy at the point of the sword and the bayonet—the work of sixty-odd negroes, many of them ignorant and depraved, together with fifty white men, outcasts of Northern society, and Southern renegades, betrayers of their race and country." To no one's surprise, the state's Black voting majority overwhelmingly approved the document. The next month, Congress likewise approved the constitution. After South Carolina's newly constituted General Assembly ratified the 14th Amendment, President Johnson in July announced that South Carolina had satisfied all congressional requirements and readmitted the state to the Union, terminating military occupation.

Voters in April also selected new representatives for the legislature set to convene in July. Elected by Williamsburg District was Stephen Swails, who resigned from the Freedmen's Bureau as he embarked on his new vocation. Republicans now controlled the state legislature in which 75 of the 124 house members were Black and twenty-five of the thirty-two senators were Republicans, ten of them Black. The newly elected governor was Robert Scott, the Republican head of South Carolina's Freedmen's Bureau.

Hopes soared in Republican circles that a new day was dawning. Much of the state's white population, however, was deeply angered at the turn of events. One disaffected citizen voiced a shared sentiment when he wrote that he had no intention of abiding by the new "negro constitution, of a negro government, establishing negro equality." The state Democratic Party petitioned Congress to reconsider its approval of the document, urging that because most of the state's voters were Black, "the effect is that the new constitution establishes in this state negro supremacy with all its train of countless evils," including subjugation of the "proud Caucasian race, whose sovereignty on earth God has ordained, and they themselves have illustrated on the most brilliant pages of the world's history." Congress, however, remained unmoved and left the South Carolina Constitution in place.

Swails's political fortunes were taking flight. Not only had Williamsburg District's voters selected him as a delegate to the constitutional convention and as a state senator, but they also elected him as district auditor. In May, Swails traveled with South Carolina's delegation to the Republican National Convention in Chicago, which nominated Ulysses S.

Grant for president by acclamation. The party's platform praised "the assured success of the reconstruction policy of Congress, as evinced by the adoption, in the majority of the States recently in rebellion, of constitutions securing equal civil and political rights to all, and regard it as the duty of the Government to sustain those constitutions, and to prevent the people of such States from being remitted to a state of anarchy or military rule." The Democratic Party, by contrast, opposed Reconstruction and urged instead that Southern states be permitted to determine their own destinies. The campaign took a decidedly racist cast when Democratic vice presidential candidate Francis Preston Blair Jr. warned that Grant's election would result in governance by "a semi-barbarous race of blacks who are worshipers of fetishes and polygamists" and were bent on "subject[ing] the white women to their unbridled lust."

In the months preceding the November 1868 election, white South Carolinians' anger turned violent. The state and country "was discovered by the white man, settled by the white man, made illustrious by the white man, and must continue to be the white man's Country," a spokesman at the Democratic Party's state convention insisted, apparently forgetting that Native Americans inhabited South Carolina thousands of years before the white man arrived. Governor Scott received daily reports that "peaceful and unoffending citizens are murdered in cold blood; ... [that] families have been forced to abandon their homes and property for fear of violence; that the authority of the State government is openly derided and denied; [and] that threats of violence, and even of death, are uttered against prominent members of the Republican party, if they attempt to visit their districts." News also reached him of large quantities of firearms smuggled into the state and "secretly distributed." All of this led Scott to conclude that there was "a systematic effort, by abuse and intimidation, to deter colored persons from the exercise of their elective franchise."

Targeted assassinations of political figures supporting equal rights for Blacks began with the killing of Solomon Dill, a white senator, former Confederate, and delegate to the constitutional convention, who had become a vocal advocate of equal treatment for all citizens regardless of race. On the night of June 4, 1868, whites gathered outside of Dill's home in Kershaw County, shot in the head an elderly Black man who came to the door, and fired into the house through the windows, killing

Dill and seriously wounding his wife. The federal prosecutor assigned to investigate the incident concluded that "the killing of Mr. Dill was a political assassination. This fact stands out in bold relief and is beyond dispute." Republicans viewed hostility from Democratic newspapers as responsible for fanning white anger into violence, citing as an example the *Charleston Courier*'s characterization of Dill as a "bitter enemy of the white race" and "an object of general loathing, execration, aversion, and hate."

Politically motivated killings of Republicans increased at a frightening pace. A few weeks after Dill's death, Republican legislator James Martin was assassinated near his hometown. Unknown assailants gunned down Johnson Stuart, a prominent Republican from Newberry, in early October, while others murdered Lee Nance in his front yard. Then on October 18, Orangeburg's Black legislator, Benjamin Franklin Randolph, whom a local newspaper accused of delivering "incendiary and threatening speeches," had just stepped from a train when three men approached on horseback, dismounted, and shot him to death. Even though the assassination occurred in broad daylight in front of multiple witnesses, no one ever identified the killers. A witness to the shooting admitted to belonging to the Ku Klux Klan and described the organization's goal as "the destruction of the Republican party and the killing or banishment of its leaders." Klansmen rode the streets at night, and reports multiplied of their beating and whipping of African Americans and threatening them with violence if they dared vote in the approaching election. Senator Swails had to focus not only on legislating but also on protecting himself and his family from disaffected whites bent on murdering them.

In an attempt to curb the violence, Governor Scott requested Wade Hampton, a former Confederate general heading the Democratic Executive Committee—"a body which represents nearly every White citizen of South Carolina," according to Hampton—to denounce the attacks and help avert a race war. Anxious to distance his party from the growing violence against Republicans, Hampton on October 23 called for an end to assassinations in a letter published by the state's Democratic committee. "We feel it our duty to invoke your earnest efforts in the cause of peace and the preservation of order," Hampton asserted, adding that the Democrats "beg you to unite with us in reprobating those recent acts of violence, resulting in the deaths of Martin, Randolph and [others], by which a few lawless and reckless men have brought discredit on the character of our people, though provocation in those cases may have been given." Concluded Hampton, "No cause can prosper which calls murder to its assistance, or which looks to assassination for success." Although attacks by the Klan abated, reports of whites intimidating Black voters continued to pour in.

This was the first presidential election in which Blacks in South Carolina could vote, and they responded to threats and intimidation by delivering Grant a resounding victory at the polls. Also for the first time, Blacks qualified to serve as presidential electors, and four African Americans did so, one from Florida and three from South Carolina. Swails, now a leading figure in South Carolina's Republican Party, was one of the three selected from that state.

On July 6, 1868, the South Carolina General Assembly convened for the first time with not only Black legislators but also a Black majority. For the next eight years, African Americans and their white Republican allies controlled the state's legislative and executive branches. During that period, Swails served as Williamsburg County's state senator, standing for election every two years and winning by "overwhelming margins" each time.

Several factors accounted for Swails's success. A sizeable majority of the county's voters were Blacks with whom he had developed close relationships as the local Freedmen's Bureau agent. Not only had he helped with housing, jobs, and disputes over labor and land contracts, but, during the run-up to the 1868 elections, he had also been in charge of distributing rations in his district. Swails was smart and educated, and because he had grown up as a free man in the North and spent most of his years engaging in a white man's world, he communicated effectively with both races. His military record with the 54th Massachusetts commanded tremendous respect; he was a war hero with the wounds to prove it and the first Black warrior commissioned as an officer in the US Army. A local historian later claimed that many of Williamsburg County's white residents were angered to learn that he had played a significant role in Potter's destructive raid through their countryside a few years earlier and disparaged him as a "carpetbagger" because of his Northern roots. No corroboration of that claim exists, however. To the contrary, Swails's Northern background and wartime experiences seem to have only increased his standing in the eyes of his constituents. A history of Williamsburg County written in 1921 with a decidedly anti-Black bias conceded that Swails was "an educated Negro" with "much natural ability" who "almost from the hour of his arrival in Williamsburg" exercised "an uncanny influence over the Negroes." A modern student of Reconstruction history deemed him "the political 'boss' of Williamsburg County."

Swails also courted the white vote in his county. Soon after moving to Kingstree, he held joint meetings with Democrats and Republicans. He moved in both Black and white political circles, which enabled him to assemble a sizeable coalition drawn from both races, allowing him to win election as Kingstree's intendant (mayor) by supporting a mix of Republican and Democratic candidates for alderman. Although his constituency was predominantly Black, it was not entirely so. Moreover, Swails studied law and in 1872 earned membership to the South Carolina bar, opening a law practice in Kingstree in 1874 with Melvin J. Hirsch, a white Jewish lawyer. In an ironic coincidence, Hirsch had fought in the war as a sergeant in the 25th South Carolina Infantry, one of the Confederate outfits engaged on James Island, where the 54th Massachusetts and Swails received their introduction to combat in July 1863.

Swails wielded substantial influence in the state senate, occupying key positions indicative of his colleagues' high regard. His fellow legislators voted him president pro tempore of the senate for six consecutive years, beginning in 1872. He chaired the senate committees on railroads and the military and served on the committees on lunatic asylums; mines and mining; railroads and internal improvements; roads, bridges, and ferries; public lands; finance; charitable institutions; the judiciary; county offices and officers; privileges and elections; immigration; and education. These were important posts that conveyed not only power and prestige but also the opportunity to dispense lucrative patronage.

The new state senator also held important Republican Party positions. He served as party chairman for the First Congressional District and Williamsburg County; a state Republican executive committeeman; Williamsburg County's representative in the state Republican convention; a delegate to the National Republican Conventions in 1868, 1872, and 1876; and a Republican presidential elector in 1868 and 1872. He founded and edited the *Williamsburg Republican,* a Kingstree newspaper that focused on issues of concern to the region's Black community. On top of this, he worked as Williamsburg County's auditor, local agent for the state land commission, and commander of the state militia. Swails also incorporated and managed several private companies, including the Savings, Building, and Loan Association of South Carolina; South Carolina Phosphate and Phosphatic River Mining Company; South Carolina Real Estate, Planning, and Mining Company; Charleston Loan and Exchange Company; Spartanburg and Port Royal Railroad; and the Anderson, Aiken, Port Royal, and Charleston Railroad. Topping it all off, Swails served as Kingstree's mayor from 1873 through 1877. He occupied the peak of Williamsburg County's political hierarchy, which even Governor Scott recognized. When Scott's private secretary referred a white office seeker to Swails, the gentleman wrote a curt letter to Scott inquiring whether Swails was the "Governor" of Williamsburg such that his approval had to be secured for any appointments.

Swails's finances were also looking up. No longer did he earn the meagre salary of a waiter or a boatman or the thirteen dollars a month the government had grudgingly paid him for soldiering. In December 1868, he bought nineteen acres and a two-story home perched on a tall brick basement on Main Street in Kingstree. He lived there with his wife, Susan, and raised their family, which soon included four children. A Black minister traveling through town reported enjoying "the hospitalities of our excellent State Senator General Swails and his happy family" and sharing "the comforts, beauty and refinements of the latest city style." Swails, he wrote, "is no doubt the most popular man in his county, a friend to our church, and our people speak of him as their greatest benefactor in assisting them in the maintenance of their liberties."

Growing violence against African Americans dominated Swails's years in the South Carolina Senate. Significantly, Williamsburg County avoided the assassinations, burnings, and intimidation that spread across the rest of the state as disaffected whites employed terror in an effort to regain control of the political process. While the county certainly experienced racial strife and significant portions of the white community opposed the growing Black political dominance, the violent eruptions experienced in neighboring counties and elsewhere were alien to Williamsburg. Swails is entitled to credit for helping keep racial discord there under control by exercising fair and thoughtful leadership and by courting support from the white community as well as from African Americans.

The Ku Klux Klan, founded in Pulaski, Tennessee, shortly after the Civil War by a handful of Confederate veterans, spread across the South in 1868 as the white populace became increasingly alarmed over the recently liberated slaves' growing political strength. In South Carolina, the Klan's interest in preserving white supremacy coincided with the Democratic Party's goal of defeating the Republicans and restoring much of the prewar social order. Working in lockstep with Democratic politicians, voter suppression became a major Klan objective. Beatings, threats of economic reprisal, and outright murder numbered among the tactics employed to keep Blacks from the voting booths.

The use of violence to regain dominance over African Americans came naturally to many white Southerners. After all, only two years had passed since most Blacks had been enslaved. Whites were accustomed to viewing them as chattels, or property, and that deeply ingrained perception did not evaporate simply because slavery had been abolished. Until recently, it was legal and proper to buy and sell Blacks, much as one would buy or sell a parcel of land or a dog. White slaveowners could separate Black husbands from their wives, sell their children to distant strangers, beat them, maim them, starve them, work them to death, or kill them immediately if they got out of hand or tried to escape. In sum, as far as Southern white culture was concerned, Blacks were not fully human, and it was acceptable—indeed, it was expected—to treat them in that spirit. If the newly liberated Black populace insisted on flexing its political muscle, violence by whites was a foreseeable response.

South Carolina's 1868 Constitution provided for a state militia. The legislature enacted the requisite legislation for it by March 1869, and recruitment began. Although a few companies were white, most were Black as the militia's prestige and pay attracted freedmen, who swelled the organization to some 100,000 members by the early 1870s. Swails's impressive military background made him an obvious choice to head the outfit. Scott initially appointed him to command a division, and in July 1873, his successor promoted Swails to major general, making him the first African American to wear two stars on his shoulders.

The state militia, however, proved ineffective. Composed largely of former slaves who had never handled firearms, it faced in the Klan a secretive paramilitary organization containing Confederate veterans seasoned by four years of combat and supported by the local white populace. Not only was the militia unable to determine in advance where the Klan and its allies might strike, but it was also outgunned on those few occasions when it actually came face to face with Klansmen. Governor Scott admitted that the force was helpless against an enemy "creating a general reign of terror and lawlessness" that was "largely composed of those who were engaged in the Confederate armies, accustomed to the use of firearms, thoroughly drilled, and armed with the most improved weapons." Militia activities also had the unintended consequence of increasing white violence, as the prospect of former slaves armed with rifles excited white citizens' deepest racial fears. A politician remarked that the predominantly Black legislature's formation of an armed militia proved that the "stupid leading darkies are determined to provoke a conflict with the white race."

In 1870, Scott ran for reelection as governor and won because of a robust Black turnout. While Republicans celebrated their victory, the state's whites concluded that electoral success by traditional means was impossible and stepped up their campaign of intimidation. Racial violence escalated dramatically, especially in South Carolina's upstate region. In Laurens County, a white mob murdered nine Republican officeholders, including a legislator, a judge, and a constable. A deputy US marshal estimated there were some five hundred shootings, beatings, and whippings in Spartanburg County, including the killing of an African American magistrate. In York County, the Klan sponsored night rides in which eleven Blacks were murdered, some six hundred were whipped, and Black schools and churches were burned. The Klan in Union County went so far as to pull Black prisoners suspected of crimes against whites from their jail cells and killed eight of them.

With the state militia powerless to stop the violence, Governor Scott petitioned Washington for assistance. In April 1871, Congress responded by passing the Ku Klux Klan Act, making it a federal crime to "conspire or go in disguise for the purpose of depriving any person or class of persons of the equal protection of the laws." The act authorized the president to suspend the writ of habeas corpus, to impose penalties, and to use military force to suppress the Klan. President Grant accordingly placed nine South Carolina counties under martial law and dispatched US troops to quell attacks against African Americans. He described the Klan's objective as employing "force and terror to prevent all political action not in accord with the view of the members; to deprive colored citizens of the right to bear arms and of the right to a free ballot; to suppress schools in which colored children were taught and to reduce the colored people to a condition closely akin to that of slavery." Federal authorities made more than a thousand arrests, but their efforts to suppress racial violence proved largely futile. The volume of cases overwhelmed prosecutors, obtaining evidence was difficult, many alleged offenses predated the law, and local juries were reluctant to convict.

The oppression of the Klan and its allies over South Carolina's freedmen cannot be overstated. "No one can imagine the sufferings these poor creatures have endured," the *New York Tribune* reported, "the terrible anxiety, the constant fear of scourging and murder, the sleeping in the woods during the cold winter nights and in the rains of spring, and the actual torture that hundreds endured whose flesh was so horribly mangled by the blows of their brutal assailants that they will never fully recover." A soldier in Spartanburg confessed that it was "impossible for me to explain the situation of this county. The KKK's, as they style themselves, have scared the people out of their wits. They are afraid to speak above a whisper."

Swails investigated several terrorist acts, including the July 1871 killing of E. J. Singletary, postmaster in Jacksville, South Carolina. According to the senator's report to Governor Scott, Singletary was walking home at night when he "was shot and instantly killed, having received seven pistol and rifle shots in the back, one pistol or rifle shot in the face, and one load of small shot in the breast." Concluded Swails, "Singletary was a native South Carolinian but an outspoken Republican which without doubt is the cause of his death."

Despite opposition from South Carolina's whites, the general assembly managed to enact legislation aimed at bettering conditions for the state's freedmen. Swails's involvement in these legislative accomplishments is not well documented, as his participation necessarily entailed informal lobbying not recorded in the state senate's records. But one white South

Carolina politician later wrote that Swails was a "very strong character and exerted considerable influence in legislation." He further identified him as taking "a very active part in all deliberations" during the 1868 Constitutional Convention and bringing that same level of engagement to his senate leadership. Swails, this politician affirmed, had been "conspicuous for [his] activity on all important legislation." And as an aside, he observed that the state senator exhibited "musical talent of a high order."

A review of the legislative records and letters to the Reconstruction governors preserved in the South Carolina Department of Archives and History reveals that Swails actively lobbied on behalf of his constituents, recommending them for positions and otherwise advancing their interests. On several occasions, he petitioned the governor to grant clemency to freedmen who had run afoul of the law. In June 1868, for example, he wrote Governor Scott seeking clemency for a fifteen-year-old boy convicted by one of Williamsburg's magistrates of stealing and killing a hog and now serving a year's sentence. Swails not only urged that the magistrate lacked authority to impose such severe punishment but also informed the governor, "it is also currently reported in the community in which the stealing was said to have been done, that the crime was never committed, and that the hog said to be killed was seen in the enclosure after the boy had been tried and sentenced."

Heading the newly elected legislature's priorities was enabling state authorities to enforce the Civil Rights Act of 1866. During discussions about this legislation, Senator Swails related how he and his Black colleagues had endured discrimination on trains, in hotels, and in billiard parlors. The law the assembly passed prohibited discrimination based on race, color, or previous condition of servitude by public or private agencies, including hotels, restaurants, and common carriers. It proved a hollow victory, however, as only one person was ever convicted of violating that law.

Education also ranked high on the legislative priority list. Slaves had received little to no schooling, which resulted in a mostly illiterate Black population, and free public education for whites had been negligible as well. The new constitution aimed to change that, mandating a public-school system free to all and funded by property and poll taxes. Scott's government went about laying its foundation, appropriating salaries, developing curriculum guidelines, drawing school-district boundaries, providing free books for indigents, and establishing a tax structure to fund the enterprise. Over the next seven years, the state's public schools grew from 400 to almost 2,800 and the teaching staff from 500 to over 3,000. Most importantly, enrollment went from 25,000 in 1869 to some 125,000 in 1874, more than half of these students African American. Again, however, reality dashed the dream. Whites were leery of educating Blacks, and the Democratic leadership encouraged them to avoid paying the poll tax, a tactic that strangled the system's funding source. Most schools could afford to stay open only a few months a year, and free textbooks were unavailable.

Admitting Blacks to South Carolina College—renamed the University of South Carolina in 1866—became an especially contentious issue. In 1869, the legislature passed an act prohibiting "any distinction in the admission of students, or the management of the college on account of race, color or creed." In practice, however, the university's student body remained white. The appointment of two Black members to the board of trustees depressed enrollment because of the white population's concern that the institution would "go up the spout, under the new regime of the Carpet bagger and Scalawags and negroes."

Those fears soon materialized. In 1873, a new board of trustees, with a majority of four Blacks—one of whom was Swails—to three whites, announced several reforms. A teacher's college opened on the campus, and the board required the university's professors to instruct those students, most of whom were African American, along with their regular university duties. Several professors resigned rather than teach Blacks, and the board fired others who opposed admitting them to the university. Then, in October, the University of South Carolina enrolled its first Black student, Henry E. Hayne, a Republican politician and the secretary of state, who hoped to earn a degree in medicine. Promptly, three members of the medical faculty resigned, and Democratic newspapers predicted the university's downfall, applauding the departing faculty for acting with "commendable dignity." Soon, virtually all of the white students had left, and the university became a predominantly Black institution. In early 1874, the legislature provided 124 scholarships to help indigent students cover living expenses while attending the school.

Writing in 1905, a historian of Reconstruction with an anti-Black sensibility deplored the "defilement" of the university by Swails and the other African Americans comprising the board's majority, rendering the institution "a mixed school for white and blacks . . . where the students of both races should intermingle on terms of actual social equality." A similar situation occurred at South Carolina's Institute for the Education of the Deaf and Blind, whose board directed that the facility not only admit Black students but also that "such pupils when admitted must be domiciled in the same building, must eat at the same table, must be taught in the same classrooms and by the same teachers, and must receive the same attention, care, and consideration as white pupils." This went too far for the institute's staff, who resigned en masse, forcing the facility to close. Democrats, of course, blamed the closure on the Republicans.

A paramount Republican challenge involved making land available to the newly freed Black constituency. The 1868 Constitution addressed the problem by calling for a Land Commission, which the legislature established in March 1869. The commission's goal was to purchase large tracts of land and to make plots ranging from twenty-five to one hundred acres available for purchase at favorable prices, with payments due over time. To prevent speculation, the commission required purchasers to occupy the land for at least three years. At first, corruption was endemic, with bribes flowing freely and acreage often purchased and distributed for reasons more political than practical. Late in 1872, however, Secretary of State Francis Cardozo was put in charge of the Land Commission and set about purging corrupt officials and instituting reforms. Ultimately, the commission enabled some 17,000 Black families and many poor whites to settle on lands it controlled. According to one count, most were unable to purchase plots, but at least 960 African Americans acquired title to property they could call their own. After Reconstruction ended, ensuing Democratic administrations ruthlessly enforced evictions, but Black ownership of land in South Carolina still outstripped that in other Southern states. "To a substantial extent," one historian noted, "Republican policy in the 1870s did fulfill the freedmen's dream of land ownership."

CHAPTER NINE

A Campaign of Intimidation and Terror

As the November 1872 election approached, the Republican Party floundered in disarray. Allegations of fraud and misuse of funds by legislators and government officials were rampant, and Governor Scott only narrowly survived an attempt to impeach him for malfeasance. Even Swails became a target of Democratic accusations. Dubbed "the great bribe taker" by newspapers with Democratic leanings, he allegedly received payments in connection with bribes related to the Land Commission and printing contracts for the legislature that received constant coverage. None of the accusations against Swails, however, ever ripened into criminal charges.

The state Republican convention in August nominated Franklin J. Moses Jr. as its candidate for governor and Richard H. Gleaves, a Black lawyer from Pennsylvania, as lieutenant governor.* A white South Carolinian, Moses advocated causes dear to the state's Black voters, including integrating the University of South Carolina, establishing a state militia, and instituting publically funded pensions for the elderly. Although he had reputedly pilfered state funds, accepted bribes, and engaged in multiple instances of corrupt behavior, Moses's strong civil rights record and his willingness to socialize with Blacks won him the nomination. Refusing to support Moses, almost a third of the delegates bolted from the convention and nominated their own candidate, who espoused

---

*Scott, who was also an attorney, remained in South Carolina until the Democrats gained control, then returned to Ohio in 1877. He was later tried in Ohio on murder charges stemming from what he claimed was the accidental discharge of his firearm, killing a young man the former governor suspected had intoxicated his son. Scott was acquitted. He died in his home in Napoleon, Ohio, in 1900.

reform and an end to government corruption. Rather than run a candidate, Democrats decided to sit out the election and watch the Republicans self-destruct.

Backed by African American voters, Moses won handily. The state's whites recoiled in horror; not only would Black interests continue to dominate state policy but a politician who in their eyes was the very personification of corruption also would be at the helm. Hampton, the Democratic Party's chairman, concluded that the time had arrived for white Southerners to "dedicate themselves to the redemption of the South." Putting the matter more bluntly, a South Carolina newspaper called upon the state's whites to stand against "the hell-born policy" that was trampling them "beneath the unholy hoofs of African savages and shoulder-strapped brigands" and subjecting them "to the rule of gibbering, louse-eating, devil worshipping, barbarians, from the jungles of Dahomey, and peripatetic buccaneers from Cape Cod, Memphremagog, Hell, and Boston."

Over the next two years, Republican fortunes rapidly declined. As the federal government became weary of investing time and money into enforcing Reconstruction, it terminated its Ku Klux Klan prosecutions and withdrew most of its troops from South Carolina, giving violent white activists—including the Redeemers, as Hampton's followers were called—a free hand to conduct their terror campaign. As predicted, corruption ran rampant, leading a foremost student of the era to conclude that Governor Moses presided over "the worse corruption and abuse in any state during Reconstruction." State expenditures skyrocketed, infuriating whites, whose taxes were paying the bills. "Millions have been stolen from the People," a disturbed citizen wrote, "to support *rogues and negroes,* and *alien* blackguards in political power—where every trace or fragment of 'States Rights' was long ago obliterated under the heel of the most *vulgar, upstart tyranny* that ever defiled the honor of a gallant nation."

The weeks leading up to the 1874 election saw the proliferation of armed white organizations, often styled as gun or rifle clubs. Moses responded by deploying new militia companies across the state, making violent confrontations inevitable. The governor pleaded for additional military assistance from Washington, but President Grant was reluctant to become more deeply involved. Swails, who stood by Moses despite

multiple corruption allegations against the governor and his administration, accompanied a delegation to Washington in April 1874 to defend
Moses and to impress the president with the need to increase, rather than
reduce, the federal military presence in South Carolina. "Swails, who is
a brigadier of militia and a nigger," a Democratic editor reported, "was
certain the troops could not be safely removed now."

In August 1874, whites occupied Georgetown, burning buildings and
firing into homes, as armed violence erupted across the state. Recognizing the need to burnish their image, Republicans in early September
broke with Moses and selected as their candidate Daniel H. Chamberlain,
a Massachusetts lawyer and former abolitionist who had served as Scott's
attorney general.* In a repeat of the previous election cycle, a conservative Republican faction founded the "Independent" Party and nominated John T. Green, a white South Carolinian, hoping to garner votes
from Democrats and disaffected Republicans. Election Day witnessed
numerous acts of violence and voter suppression, but the party's Black
base held firm and elected Chamberlain governor.

Results in national elections, however, spelled disaster for the Republicans. For the first time in over a decade, they lost the House of Representatives, diminishing still further the possibility of federal intervention
in South Carolina and in the other Southern states. A brutal national
economic depression, dissention among various Republican factions,
and a series of scandals seriously eroded the national party's enthusiasm
for Reconstruction and diminished its willingness to continue sending
troops and spending money to ensure civil rights in the South. A Democratic commentator observed that his party's national election victory
was "hailed with Thanksgiving in South Carolina, as an indication that
the North had determined to protest against the oppression of the Southern whites by their old slaves and the carpet-baggers."

Hoping to broaden his electoral base, Chamberlain set about introduc-
ing reforms to eliminate corruption and to signal to Democrats that he
was willing to cooperate with them. Many of South Carolina's conserva-

*Moses left South Carolina and suffered through a miserable existence. He abandoned
his wife, stole from his mother, was arrested in several states for theft, and spent three
years in jail in Massachusetts, where he blamed his misconduct on addiction to cocaine.
He died in December 1906 in a rooming house in Winthrop, Massachusetts.

tive newspapers applauded his proposals, and he received invitations to speak at chambers of commerce and other institutions generally hostile to Republican politicians. But the Republican-led legislature, whose Black majority was in no mood to placate its white opponents, sabotaged his efforts to change the course of state politics. In the governor's absence, the legislators selected Moses and William J. Whipper, a Black Pennsylvanian suspected of gross malfeasance, as circuit-court judges. Chamberlain denounced the appointments as "a horrible disaster" and refused to approve them out of concern that he would irreparably alienate Democrats. "Unless the universal opinion of all who are familiar with his character are mistaken, [Moses] is as infamous a character as ever in any age disgraced and prostituted public position," Chamberlin wrote in explaining the situation to President Grant. "The character of W. J. Whipper," he continued, "differs from that of Moses only in the extent to which opportunity has allowed him to exhibit it." The damage, however, had been done. As Chamberlain feared, whites were outraged over the general assembly's judicial choices. "Moses shall never take his seat as Judge in our Courthouse unless placed there by Federal bayonets," an editorial insisted.

With the 1876 election season looming on the horizon, white South Carolina united in opposition to Black rule. "A minority of white men, when united in a common purpose, never fails to drive from power a semi-barbarous majority," the editor of the *Greenville News* asserted, insisting that the white race "will not be negroized, but will perish foot by foot, inch by inch, before it will consent to be mongrelized." White citizens rallied across the state, and racial violence escalated. On July 4, white anger erupted when a Black militia unit in the village of Hamburg blocked a public street and permitted two white travelers to pass only after a hostile confrontation. A few days later, a white mob seeking its version of immediate justice stormed a warehouse where the militiamen had assembled, blasted an entryway with a cannon, and captured most of the Blacks huddling inside. After murdering six of the prisoners, they ordered the remaining captives to run and shot at them as well. Several white participants were charged with the murders, but none were convicted.

The Republican Party was seriously divided, and Chamberlain, facing growing opposition, struggled to remain at the helm. Matters came to a head when the Republicans met on April 11, 1876, to determine whether he should lead the state's delegation to the Republican National Convention. As the discussion became heated, one of Chamberlain's supporters—Judge "Tom" Mackey, a white man—shouted: "Gentlemen of the convention, the only question before us is whether the respectable and honest minority of the Republican Party of this State, headed by Governor Chamberlain, shall obtain their rights, or whether they shall be deprived of those rights by men whom I now denounce, in the presence of high heaven, as the thieves and rascals who have brought disgrace and shame upon the party in South Carolina."

Swails, standing next to him, immediately demanded, "To whom do you apply that language, Judge Mackey?"

"To you, Sir for one," Mackey snarled in reply. "You are one of them, and today we send all of you to everlasting defeat. You have come here to trample on the honest people of South Carolina. We can send you all to jail, and we mean to do it."

"You are a damned liar," Swails shouted back. Sensing that a fight was about to erupt, delegates rushed to separate the two men. Robert Brown Elliott, a prominent African American attorney and Speaker of the Assembly, stood directly in front of Mackey, a small desk between them. Looking him straight in the eye, Elliott demanded: "Do you mean to say that the majority of the delegates here are thieves?"

"I mean to say that there is a band of robbers in South Carolina," Mackey shot back, "and that you, Sir, are their chief!"

"Elliott's black face became pale with rage, and without a word he drew his revolver," a newspaper correspondent stationed within feet of the two men reported. "This was the only signal which seemed to be needed, and in an instant half a dozen pistols were out," he related. Another reporter stared in astonishment as "tables were upset in all directions, [and] a chair was brandished over the head of Chamberlain, who sat unmoved." Several newspaper correspondents "who were directly in the way of the combatants held them back for a moment, and until they were more effectually separated by a number of the cooler delegates. None of the pistols were discharged, but both Elliott and Mackey were severely shaken by the crowd which separated them. Elliott's wife, who was in the ladies' gallery, seeing the pistols drawn, rushed screaming through the hall. Other women followed her example, and what with the yells of the maddened negroes and the cries of the women, the scene was almost indescribable."

Once order was restored, the meeting turned to select a temporary chairman. Both Chamberlain and Swails received nominations for the position, and the matter went to a vote. Swails won, receiving eighty votes to Chamberlain's forty. There could have been no clearer demonstration that Swails still commanded the respect and support of the legislature's Black majority.

The next day, Chamberlain delivered an hour-and-a-half-long speech that alleviated much of the divisiveness, and the delegates overwhelmingly chose him to lead the South Carolina delegation to the Republican National Convention. Swails, of course, accompanied him as a delegate.

In September, the state's Republicans met to select a candidate for governor and chose Chamberlain, who had Swails's backing, to run for a second term, but only after he agreed to accept his rival, Robert Elliott, as his running mate. The bargains he struck with corrupt legislators to secure the nomination cost him the support of moderates, who now viewed Chamberlain as having compromised his ethics to win the election.

Democrats, meanwhile, nominated Hampton for the governorship. From their perspective, he had an impeccable pedigree as a white Southern stalwart, and voters of all classes seemed drawn to him. Born into a wealthy South Carolina plantation family, Hampton had served in the state senate before the war, volunteered as a private in the Confederate military, and ultimately won promotion as a lieutenant general after successfully commanding Lee's cavalry corps. "He was a big, powerful, athletic man," a correspondent covering the election reported, "with rather small dark blue eyes, the face of a good humored, self-confident, fearless fighter, carrying just enough extra flesh to become his fifty-eight years." Hampton's speeches were "just plain, straight talks," he "never became excited or shouted or gesticulated," but he was not beyond injecting a little spontaneous humor. At one rally, an attractive young woman pulled a watch from her bosom and exclaimed, "Oh, my watch has stopped!" Without missing a beat, Hampton replied, "That is very natural, for I am sure had I been in the watch's place, I would have stopped too."

Hoping to attract reform-minded Republicans and some Blacks to his cause, Hampton espoused a relatively moderate platform and urged an end to violence. Many of his followers, egged on by another former Confederate cavalry general, Martin W. Gary, saw things differently. The result was a dual strategy, with Hampton taking a moderate tact and reaching out to Black voters, while other Democrats pursued a policy of threats and intimidation. "Treat them as to show them you are the Superior race, and that their natural position is that of subordination to the white man," Gary advised his adherents of the approach they should take with Black voters. "Never threaten a man individually," he suggested, but "if he deserves to be threatened, the necessity of the times require that he should die." Coercion became a major theme of the Democrats' election strategy, administered by rifle-club members clad in flannel shirts dyed red. "Red Shirts," as they were called, made it a point to attend Republican events, firing guns and terrorizing participants. Several encounters turned bloody, leading President Grant to denounce the "insurrection" and "domestic violence" in South Carolina. At Governor Chamberlain's urging, Grant transferred 1,100 US soldiers to the state, threatening force unless the rifle clubs disbanded. The violence continued, however, aimed at giving Black citizens a taste of what they could expect if they dared go to the polls.

In mid-September, Hampton began a six-week tour through the state, delivering scores of speeches and meeting thousands of voters. The tenor of these spectacles, an historian later noted, "was not that of a candidate or a challenger; rather, it resembled the triumphant procession of a conquering hero." Crowds greeted him at every stop, bands played, and theatrics took center stage. Arriving in Sumter, he walked into the town square, where a woman lay on the ground wearing a ribbon stating, "South Carolina." Hampton lifted her, and the crowd erupted in cheers. On another occasion, he mounted a stage lined with smiling young girls representing each state and a single downcast girl dressed in mourning and draped in chains. As Hampton approached, the girl's chains and mourning robes fell away, and she transformed into a "radiant young woman," head held high and eyes beaming with excitement, sporting a golden coronet on her head emblazoned with the name "South Carolina." The crowd went wild, and Hampton broke into tears.

During late October and early November, Democrats held rallies in counties across the state. A major attraction at these events included a procession of each county's whites, led by the local Democratic chairman and his staff followed by hundreds—sometimes thousands—of mounted Red Shirts. "A thousand men on horseback, riding in easy order, every man yelling as long as his throat could stand the effort," a writer recounted, "the route to the speaking ground lined with men, women and children, waving flags or hats or handkerchiefs to the riders and doing their part to increase the lusty yells and defiant hurrahs" made a stirring scene. On reaching the speaking grounds, the ranks would open, and Hampton, accompanied by local officials clad in Red Shirts, would walk to the stand and give a rousing oration.

Violence against Blacks continued unabated. Trial Justice E. J. Black in Blackville, a small town in Barnwell County, investigated the murder of a field hand killed by a party of mounted whites while picking cotton. Concluding that the incident was but one of many, he wrote Governor Chamberlain about the "truly deplorable" situation in his part of the state. "The colored people are being shot in all sections of this county for their political opinions," he reported. "We hear of someone being killed every day. Armed bands of mounted men are raising about the country every night, threatening colored people. There are now about forty refugees here having been driven from their homes by these armed bands which are no other than the Rifle Clubs of this county."

Election Day witnessed numerous instances of voter intimidation. Armed Red Shirts visited polling places to frighten Black voters away and to remind them of the consequences if they persisted in trying to vote. According to the Democratic Party's instructions, poll workers must challenge every Negro but "vote every white man who is willing to vote." The party further advised, "we must have someone for clerk who can cook the record," suggesting, "if toward the close of day you find that they have the majority, stuff the box. If they are very much in majority make two boys load their pistols with blank cartridge and get up a fight at the box, shoot in good earnest if a Negro is impertinent, but shoot straight and hit a leader and if once hit be sure to finish him." Riots erupted in Charleston, and allegations of fraud, such as whites casting multiple ballots, were widespread.

Election returns suggested that Hampton had won by a narrow margin, receiving 92,261 votes to Chamberlain's 91,127. But in two counties—Edgefield and Laurens—the Democratic vote significantly exceeded the number of eligible voters, casting the returns in those coun-

124 – STEPHEN A. SWAILS

ties into doubt. Republicans, of course, contested the results, throwing the question of who had won into limbo. Compounding the confusion, the two parties disagreed over whether the State Board of Canvassers or the General Assembly had authority to resolve the dispute. The state supreme court decided that the board should tabulate the votes but that the legislature should determine the results. The board, however, declared the election invalid, which prompted the court to hold the commissioners in contempt and order their arrest.

Meanwhile, Chamberlain persuaded federal soldiers to occupy the statehouse and admit only legislators certified by the secretary of state or the board, which excluded those from Edgefield and Laurens Counties. Protestors mobbed the statehouse, and Chamberlain, fearing more violence, asked Hampton to help calm the situation. Hampton hurried to the statehouse, mounted the steps, and asked the mob to disperse. As most of the protestors supported the Democrat, they did as he asked.

Returns for state senators indicated a small Republican majority, which no one contested. In Williamsburg County, Swails won again, and the senate once more elected him as its president pro tempore. The house, however, presented an entirely different picture, as the questionable Edgefield and Laurens results led each party to claim victory. When the Republicans insisted that they had won and proceeded to choose a speaker, the Democrats walked out, pronounced themselves the real victors, and picked their own speaker. The situation deteriorated even further when the Democrats returned to the house chamber. For several days, the two speakers stood side by side at the podium, trying to outshout one another. Brawls and arguments among legislators—"at one time it seemed that bloodshed was imminent," a witness remarked—completed the scene of utter pandemonium.

The contested governorship fared no better. On December 5, Republicans in both chambers rejected the returns from the two disputed counties, declared Chamberlain the winner, and inaugurated him two days later. An enraged Hampton announced, "The people have elected me Governor, and, by the Eternal God, I will be Governor or we shall have a military governor." The following week, the General Assembly's Democrats voted to accept the returns from the disputed districts, declared Hampton the winner, and inaugurated him. South Carolina now had two rival governments.

The national presidential race was almost as chaotic. Democratic candidate Samuel Tilden had won the popular vote over Republican Rutherford B. Hayes, but the Electoral College had yet to proclaim who had won. The contested results in South Carolina further complicated matters, as Chamberlain certified that Hayes had carried the state, while the Democrats claimed that Tilden had won. To break the deadlock, Hayes agreed on a compromise with congressional Democrats. In exchange for their acquiescence in his election, he would acknowledge their control of the South, end Reconstruction, and agree to serve only one term as president. On March 2, 1877, the Electoral College declared Hayes the victor, his 185 electoral votes trumping Tilden's 184. On March 5, Hayes became president of the United States, and Reconstruction soon came to an end.

In the meantime, Hampton resorted to a "starve them out" policy, telling his followers to stop paying taxes to Chamberlain's government and to send 10 percent of their taxes to Hampton's faction instead. Because most of the state's affluent taxpayers were Democrats, the tactic was effective. Even lame-duck president Grant agreed that, "unless Governor Chamberlain can compel the collection of taxes, it will be utterly useless for him to expect to maintain his authority for any length of time."

On March 22, in an effort to resolve South Carolina's impasse, the newly installed Hayes invited Chamberlain and Hampton to Washington and tried to hammer out a compromise. Failing to persuade them to agree, the president, in the spirit of the deal he had struck with the Democrats, washed his hands of the matter. The federal government, he announced, loathed to become involved in internal state squabbles and would withdraw all US troops from South Carolina.

At noon on April 10, the last contingent of federal troops departed the state. The national government having withdrawn its support, Chamberlain saw no route to victory. "By the order of the President whom your votes alone rescued from overwhelming defeat," he bitterly informed his African American supporters, "the government of the United States abandons you . . . with full knowledge that the lawful government of the state will be speedily overthrown." Denouncing Hayes's betrayal, Chamberlain mourned that the same Republican Party that had liberated the slaves had now abandoned the freedmen to rule by "that class at the South which regard slavery as a Divine Institution, which waged four years of destructive war for its perpetuation, [and] which steadily opposed citizenship and suffrage for the negro."

The next day, Chamberlain agreed to surrender the governor's office to Hampton, and at noon, his secretary handed over the keys to the Democrat. "The troops have been withdrawn, and Chamberlain surrenders South Carolina," Hampton telegraphed a supporter. Reconstruction and Republican control of South Carolina were over. As W. E. B. Du Bois later aptly put it, "The slave went free, stood a brief moment in the sun, then moved back again towards slavery."*

Democrats swiftly moved to consolidate their power. Hampton was now governor, and William D. Simpson, a prominent Democratic politician and former Confederate officer, became lieutenant governor. Simpson also became the senate's president and immediately seated four Democratic senators-elect whose victories had been contested. Machinations in the house enabled Democrats to secure a majority there as well. A special legislative session in April repealed a law providing pensions to the widows and families of political-violence victims and an act providing scholarships to help needy students attend the state college. They also formed a joint committee to investigate alleged corruption and misdeeds during the Republican years. "The primary purpose of the legislative committee was to blacken the reputation of those who governed the state from 1868 to 1877," historian Walter Edgar concluded, and "in that, the committee succeeded." It produced reports claiming multiple instances of fraud, which led to formal charges against some twenty officials— Swails not among them—and convictions of three. Intimidated by the investigations, several Republican senators resigned. In short order, the Democrats removed Republican judges and replaced them with more sympathetic followers. They now controlled the state government's executive, legislative, and judicial branches.

Democrats also moved methodically to ensure victory in the approaching 1878 election, redrawing congressional districts to neutralize the concentration of Black voters in the state's Low Country. They

---

*Chamberlain relocated to New York City, where he practiced law and taught constitutional law at Cornell University. After a profitable legal career, he traveled throughout Europe before finally settling in Charlottesville, Virginia, where he died in April 1907.

also abolished voting precincts in areas that contained Republican majorities, in some instances compelling Black voters to walk twenty or more miles and cross wide rivers to vote. The campaign of terror and intimidation continued unabated, with Swails a favorite target. "Troops of red-shirts have ridden up to his home," the *New York Times* reported, "uttering fierce rebel yells and applying most opprobrious epithets to him, the presence of his wife and family not being heeded."

On November 27, 1877, the legislature convened for its fall session, and Swails, along with nine other Republicans, resigned from the senate. Reporting the resignations, the *Newberry Weekly Herald* noted, "Swails is a mulatto carpet-bagger, who has been one of the most prominent Republicans in the State since 'reconstruction.'" The former senator settled into life in Kingstree, raising his family, practicing law, editing his newspaper, and remaining a major force in Republican politics.

As election time approached, the state's Republicans faced an uphill battle. Democrats not only controlled the three branches of government but had also stacked the cards in their favor by redrawing voting districts, closing critical voting precincts, and placing Democrats in charge of recording and counting votes. To make matters worse, the federal government had abandoned the state's Republicans, leaving them at the mercy of the Klan and the Red Shirts. South Carolina's Republicans wallowed in "apathy, fear, and defeatism engendered by [the Democrat's campaign to control the election] and President Hayes's betrayal."

A reporter covering the upcoming elections observed that Democrats had "organized a campaign of intimidation and terror which is even more extensive and systematic than was the infamous canvas of 1876." Even as he was writing his piece, the newspaperman noted, "there come through my window the sound of men drilling in the streets." He witnessed Red Shirts parading regularly, making Republican gatherings too dangerous to attend. "Whenever the colored people attempt to come together they are surrounded by armed white men, who are always on hand for the purpose."

At their state convention in August 1878, South Carolina's Republicans hotly debated how best to respond to the Democrats' advantages. Several delegates argued that they should not contest Hampton's reelection and instead focus on winning the races for local and legislative positions, reasoning that this strategy would lull the Democrats into withholding their formidable resources against Republicans running for lower-level offices. Swails, who attended as Williamsburg County's delegate, took a contrary position and urged the convention to launch a full-scale attack against the entire Democratic ticket. Those opposing a full offensive prevailed—a decision the party's platform explained by noting that Democratic tactics hindered the Republicans' ability to effectively organize "without incurring great personal danger."

With the Republican Party opting to forgo a race against Hampton, Swails devoted his efforts to energizing support for local candidates. He was by far "the most prominent Republican and the best political worker in Williamsburg County," a correspondent for the *New York Times* reported. "In defiance of repeated warnings, he made a determined effort to organize his party and bring out the vote. He was obliged to work in secret, however. He dared not call public meetings, but in the by-ways, in the swamps and woods, addressed the little bands of Republicans who came to hear him." As Swails had earlier cautioned, "you cannot speak without a guard if you are a Republican." But he became bolder as the campaign progressed and announced a Republican meeting at White Oak, a crossroads settlement north of Kingstree.

Swails and A. J. M. Montgomery, who participated in the meeting at White Oak, left detailed accounts of what happened there. On Saturday, May 5, Swails, his young son, and Montgomery traveled to Elijah Chapel in White Oak to address a Republican club. Soon after they arrived, a wagon carrying several white Democrats from Kingstree—including Purvis Nelson, J. S. Hayward, and Thomas Gilland—drew up to the church. When Nelson walked inside, the club's chairman, Thomas Wilson, ordered him to leave, as this was a Republican meeting. Nelson demanded equal time to address the assembly, but Wilson denied him permission. Nelson then left.

Swails addressed the club members, reminding them that "we must stand together, shoulder to shoulder, elbow to elbow, and we will surely win on the 5th of November." He cautioned against rioting, emphasizing that "you must be law abiding citizens," no matter what wrongful action the Democrats attempted. "Two wrongs cannot make one right," he stressed.

Montgomery spoke next, but he had hardly begun when Nelson and his companions stormed into the church and demanded an opportunity to speak. "He seemed to be somewhat under the influence of liquor, and commenced speaking about having fair play and dividing time," Swails recalled. "Finding that Nelson intended to make a disturbance, I advised the President of the club to adjourn the meeting, which he did, the members leaving for their homes."

Swails, his son, Montgomery, and six or seven other Republicans started back toward Kingstree. About a mile from White Oak, a crowd of some one hundred men overtook their group. These men were armed and seemed to Swails to belong to Captains Thomas M. Gilland's, Hugh Cooper's, and William J. Fitch's companies of state militia. One of the county election commissioners, Dr. O. D. M. Byrd, commanded the entire outfit.

After trailing Swails and his companions for a while, Byrd's command divided into two detachments, one of which passed the Republicans and rode in front of them. They all continued in silence until about two miles from Kingstree, when the lead detachment halted and formed across the roadway. Byrd then approached Swails and proposed that he ride in front. "This I declined to do," Swails later wrote of the incident, "stating to him that I was then on my way home; that I had gone peaceably and attended to my business and was now returning."

Montgomery, who was with Swails, heard the entire exchange and recalled it as follows:

Dr. Byrd: "You have done a great deal of harm in this County and I propose to take care of you."
Swails: "I am on my way peacefully for home and do not want any riot to occur here today."
Dr. Byrd: "You get in front of the ranks Swails."
Swails: "And I do not mean to do it unless I am taken by violence."
Dr. Byrd: "If everybody is of my sentiment, you will be taken by violence."
Dr. Byrd's companions: "That's my sentiment!"
Swails: "Am I and my men to be considered under arrest?"
Dr. Byrd: "Yes."

Swails realized that resistance was futile. "Go on," he told Byrd. "I will go to the village with you." When several of Byrd's men approached Swails and seemed about to draw their pistols, he and his companions started down the road toward Kingstree. On approaching town, Byrd directed the procession to proceed right onto Academy Street, as though he intended for them to march around the village. Swails, however, continued straight ahead on Main Street toward the center of town, surrounded by militiamen screaming threats. As he approached the courthouse, his friend Reverend E. M. Pinckney urged him to dismount and seek shelter there. Swails dismounted and headed into the building, but Byrd and another man seized him to prevent him from entering. Reverend Pinckney and another man, Boson Hanna, also grabbed their friend, wrestled him from Byrd, and pulled him into the courthouse entryway.

Two shots rang out—according to Swails, Dr. Byrd fired one of the shots—wounding Hanna in his right breast and left thigh. Sheriff Jacobs, another of Swails's friends, ran into the passage and ordered the crowd to disperse, while Trial Justice Steele, who was also present, watched but said nothing. The sheriff's intervention, however, persuaded the militiamen to leave. After they were gone, Swails returned home without further incident.

The following Tuesday, Swails visited the courthouse on business, and soon a crowd of Red Shirts began assembling outside. Concerned, he hurried home and drafted a letter to Judge Wallace, urging him to forbid the Red Shirts from gathering around the courthouse. Suddenly, several members of the Democratic Executive Committee appeared at his front door, barged into his home, and read aloud from a set of resolutions they asserted the committee and several prominent members of the community had passed. According to Reverend Pinckney, who was with Swails and made notes as the men spoke, the resolutions provided:

1. *Resolved:* That S. A. Swails be required to leave Williamsburg in 10 days
2. *Resolved:* That he is a high-handed robber
3. *Resolved:* That he and his rioters be held responsible for all incendiarism which may happen
4. *Resolved:* That unless the above be complied with he must forfeit his life

According to Swails, "these men came into my house unbidden, and read the threats in the presence of my wife." Pinckney later delivered a copy of the resolutions to Judge Wallace, who promised that he would "attend to it." Later, the judge summoned Swails and explained that he could do nothing about the resolutions. "The upshot of what he said was that I could not be protected," Swails later wrote, "that neither he nor Hampton could protect me, unless I would renounce my Republican principles. He said he had no authority to order the band of men out of the village. They had a constitutional right to bear arms. When by the beating of a drum they had disturbed his court he had a right to interfere, but he had none when they interfered with me. He told me plainly that neither he nor Gov. Hampton could control these men."

That evening, Swails traveled by rail to Charleston on business. On his return, a crowd of Red Shirts met him at the depot shouting, "Good-bye Swails," followed by a string of expletives. Reverend Pinckney and other of Swails's friends advised him not to get off the train. He decided to continue to Washington, "my object being to make known the methods taken by the Democrats of my State to get rid of Republican minorities."

Swails also asked Pinckney for a copy of the resolutions that the Democratic Executive Committee had brought to his house. The reverend approached the committee's secretary, a Mr. Kelly, who refused to give him a copy. Pinckney tried again, then relayed Kelly's response to Swails. "Mr. Kelly told me today that Gov. Hampton sanctioned what they were doing," Pinckney wrote, "and the killing of Swails would take place if he remained here after 10 days."

CHAPTER TEN

What a Mockery of Justice Is This?

On October 14, 1878, Swails, accompanied by South Carolina congressman Joseph H. Rainey—the first African American member of Congress
and a former slave—met with President Hayes in Washington. The
Janesville Daily Gazette in Wisconsin reported that Swails, "a resolute
man, nearly white," informed the president "of the atrocious and lawless
conduct of these unterrified Democrats, sanctioned by Gov. Hampton
and his conciliated advisers." According to the *New York Times,* the two
men also told him that "the Democrats, uniformed in Red Shirts, armed
with state guns and led by prominent officers of the state government,
interfered with the Republicans and prevented them from assembling
peaceably to listen to addresses from their leaders." Swails added that
he had been "forced to fly from his home because of the activity in organizing and addressing Republican meetings." Hayes responded that
he would forward the matter to his attorney general with instructions
to take such action as the facts and law permitted. "Mr. Swails called
the attention of the President to an editorial in the Columbia *Register*
bidding defiance to the Federal authorities, and to a similar editorial
in the Charleston *News and Courier,* and the President appeared to be
deeply impressed with the facts set forth," the *Gazette* reported. When
Swails asked the president what he should tell people back in South
Carolina, Hayes lamely replied, "Tell them that they have all the protection the law shall give."

Democratic newspapers put their own spin on Swails and Rainey's
visit with President Hayes. "This man Swails was for a long time president pro tem of the South Carolina Senate under the carpet-bag regime
and was one of the most audacious of the crew that fattened on the unfor-

tunate state," the *Baltimore Sun* reported. "The committee on frauds of the Hampton Legislature examined into his conduct, and he was allowed to resign as State Senator." He returned to Williamsburg County, the account claimed, which he had "misrepresented" for years, "and immediately set to work to array the blacks against the whites." According to the newspaper, "He gathered the blacks together in midnight meetings, denounced the whites in violent language, and gave his followers violent and incendiary counsel, but was tolerated by the people of Williamsburg county until they were in daily and hourly fear not only of their property but of their lives." They ordered him to leave, the *Sun*'s story continued, and he immediately rushed to Washington and, joined by Congressman Rainey, secured an audience with the president. The reporter speculated that Rainey "allowed his better judgment to be overcome" by supporting Swails "for the reason probably that his chances of election are exceedingly slim by reason of so many of the colored people joining the democratic party." Swails and Rainey's story of intimidation, the Democrats insisted, "were from persons notoriously unworthy of confidence, and who are loath to abandon the occupation of stirring up strife between the two races, it having become second nature with them."

South Carolina's attorney general, Judge Leroy F. Youmans—who at the 1865 Constitutional Convention had opposed ending slavery—on October 21 met with President Hayes to set the record straight. According to the *Washington Post*'s October 25 coverage of the meeting, the object of his visit was to refute the "slanders" that the "gang of copper-colored conspirators have entertained the administration with." Youmans explained that the "outrages" alleged by Swails and his coconspirators were "entirely without foundation, and had been started and circulated by designing persons for political effect." Swails and his "small clique of designing Radicals" were not to be believed, the judge urged the president. "In the palmy days of carpet-bagism these men figured among the most unscrupulous knaves who robbed the State, and some of them have been branded by the courts as common felons," he claimed, and "they are now seeking to play the same game which told with such effect in former years; they raise the cry of oppression and outrage upon the colored people, and spread lies broadcast through the country to make political capital." According to the *Intelligencer* in Anderson, South Carolina,

Youmans's "simple statement is enough to overthrow the sworn evidence of a thousand such as Swails [and others] and their gang."

Judging from the extensive Northern newspaper coverage, Swails actively courted the press to counter the Democrats' version of events. In a statement printed in Cincinnati and Indianapolis, he explained that even though South Carolina, based on its demographics, should elect five Republican congressmen, intimidation and violence by the Democrats made that impossible. "Although the Republicans have large majorities in all districts, such is the terrorism prevailing and the resolve of the democrats to employ all machinery against them, I am satisfied they will be successful," Swails told the newspapers. "The Republicans of my state feel that they have been deserted, and I cannot blame them for refusing to jeopardize their lives."

Swails also told the press about transgressions by his successor in the state senate, Samuel W. Maurice, chairman of the Williamsburg County Democratic Party and editor of the *Kingstree Star*. Allegedly, Maurice had demanded that Swails tell him "the exact time in which he (Swails) will leave for good, and beyond which he will not be allowed to stay." He had further threatened that Swails resided in Kingstree "at his personal risk, and that his permanently remaining here will not be permitted by the whites of the county." A Boston newspaper carrying this account observed that its readers could "judge how far the rights of the colored are respected by the Constitution-loving democratic party of the South under such leadership. Many of the leaders of that party in South Carolina are as rank with treason today as they were before the war."

Swails also wrote Hampton that mounted Red Shirts had arrested him while returning from a Republican meeting and had ordered him to leave the state "forthwith upon peril to his life." Describing the ordeal at some length, he closed by observing:

it has come to a point that a man cannot be happy to be a Republican and should be assailed in open, broad daylight today under the portals of the temple of justice, and the eyes of the sworn peace officers of the State. Sir, I am confident that you would not so forget your high office and your solemn oath as Chief Magistrate of the State to sympathize at such outrageous [acts] or allow them to go unpunished. I would state that there has been so many troubles among the colored people of this County but they have hitherfore born insult and jibes without asserting themselves and peacefully and quietly and in fair name and on behalf I ask that the affairs be fully investigated.

Hampton replied with a response made public in the *Charleston News and Courier*:

While I depreciate [sic] all acts of violence and am always willing to exert proper authority in maintaining laws, you must recognize that I have no power to exercise judicial authority nor to take cognizance of such offenses as fall under the jurisdiction of legal tribunals. If the facts you state are correct, the parties who stopped and arrested you on a public highway were guilty of a grave offense, and it is your duty to have them indicted. The courts are open to all citizens, and all can secure justice before them. The only matter that I can with propriety act upon is the charge made against Trial Justice Steele, and this shall be fully investigated. All my efforts during this canvass have been used to promote harmony and preserve the peace. If there should occur any public disturbance where I could properly act, all of the authority of my office shall be used to quell it, and to give full protection to all citizens of the state. I have no sympathy with lawlessness of any sort, nor with those who seek to produce discord between the two races.

Respectfully yours,
Wade Hampton

P.S. In justice to Trial Justice Steele I ask you prefer specific charges against him. In the meantime, I refer your letter to Solicitor Hirsch, requesting him to investigate the whole matter and report to me. You can communicate with him.

Denouncing Hampton's reply as a "direct and notorious falsehood," one Pennsylvania newspaper expressed grave doubts that Republicans could obtain justice in South Carolina's courts. "The outrages against Mr. Swails, including the shooting of one of his companions, are acknowledged by the local organ of Governor Hampton to be all that Swails represents them," the newspaper observed. "Swails himself is a refugee in Washington, with a threat of death hanging over him if he returns. Yet Governor Hampton pleads his inability to protect him, and advises him to seek redress through the courts; or, in other words, at the hands of the very men who committed the crimes against him. What a mockery of justice is this?"

The *New York Times* was especially scathing in its analysis of Hampton's letter. "To tell Republican sufferers that the courts are open to them, and that it is their duty to have their assailants indicted, is, in the circumstances, a cheap method of keeping up appearances," the newspaper fumed. "H[ampton] knows that the Democratic managers pull the judicial wires, and that the Republican who dares to ask for their indictment is arrested and hurried off on charges trumped up for the occasion. If he has 'no sympathy for lawlessness of any sort,' why does he consent to play the game of those who rely on lawlessness for the attainment of Democratic success?" Hampton, the *Times* concluded, was nothing more than a "tool of an ultra partisanship that strives to reimpose the yoke of bondage on colored people and turns backward the movement of the State. The personal humiliation involved in this condition of affairs is a matter that belongs to himself. But in these facts we have the key to the self-stultification and the thinly-disguised hypocrisy of the letter we print today."

Compounding Hampton's hypocrisy was the fact that Solicitor Hirsch, charged by the governor with investigating the allegations, was none other than Swails's estranged former law partner, Melvin Hirsch. The previous May, the two lawyers had quarreled bitterly, and their differences culminated in personal attacks in the local newspaper. "As you have seen fit to attack me, partly through the columns of the paper, I shall take the liberty at some time to reply thereto," Hirsch had written Swails on May 20, 1877. "Feeling that this step of yours exhibits none of the best feelings toward me, I deem it due to myself to withdraw from the law partnership now existing, the same to take effect from the first day of May, 1877, all business now in our hands will be continued to a termination."

Hirsch's report was as negative as Swails predicted. "As I expected and as I told Governor Hampton, the fact of it is Hirsch has done what the Governor wished him to do, viz., white-wash the action of the parties engaged in the affairs and at the same time, lie only," Swails wrote after reviewing the document. "I can hardly imagine how any man could allow himself to be used as such a political machine. Hirsch knows full well that the so-called Committee of Safety who called on me was the Democratic Executive Committee of the County."

In the meantime, the district attorney's office issued arrest warrants for sixteen persons charged with "interfering with Swails in his advocacy of Rainey for Congress at the White Oak meeting" and with "giving Swails notice to leave the county." Among the defendants were Dr. Byrd and company commanders Fitch, Gilland, and Cooper. They appeared in court on October 24 and were released on bond. Ultimately, the cases went nowhere, as Hirsch's investigation found no criminal conduct.

While Swails remained in Washington waiting in vain for a federal response to his complaints, November 5, 1878—Election Day—came and went. The results were as expected. Running unopposed, Hampton was reelected governor, and Democratic legislative candidates swept the state, even in Williamsburg County, which was overwhelmingly Black and Republican. "The Democrats refused the United States Supervisor admission to the polls, and in the evening seized the ballot box and stuffed it," Swails's friend Reverend Pinckney explained. A Black election official confirmed that "there were more ballots in the box than names on the poll-list, and one of the Democratic clerks was at work throughout the night adding names to the poll-list to make the numbers agree."

Later that month, Zebulon White of the *New York Tribune* interviewed the *Kingstree Star*'s editor about the recent election. When asked why the county, in which Blacks outnumbered whites two to one, had elected a Democratic representative, the editor suggested that "some of the niggers voted the Democratic ticket." When asked if there had been much excitement during the campaign, he said that there had been some trouble in Kingstree and explained:

"We gave Swails ten days to leave, and he left. Everything was quiet after that."

"Who is Swails?" correspondent White asked.

"He is a nigger from the North," the editor responded. "From Pennsylvania I reckon. He has been State Senator for this County."

"What had Swails been doing," inquired White.

"Playing devil with the niggers; making incendiary speeches."

"Was he a man of influence among them?"

"Yes, he could do anything he pleased with them."

"What effect did his going away have on the negroes?"

"It broke them up—they had no leader any more."

Interested in seeing whether Swails had actually benefited Kingstree's Black populace, White toured the town, where he was impressed by the "colored children, thirty or forty of them, intelligent-looking, well-dressed, decorously-behaved, carrying their satchels and books." Heading into the countryside, he found that "more than half the land for the first eight miles, on both sides of the road, and within one or two miles of it, had been purchased by negroes during the past five or six years, and that most of it had been paid." The white population might view Swails as the devil, but the benefits that the county's African Americans had gained was starkly evident.

Threats against him from South Carolina's Democrats continued, persuading Swails to remain in Washington for his personal safety. To make ends meet, he obtained work as a clerk in the Post Office Department and wrote his friend, Sheriff Jacobs, asking him to send his horse equipment. "I went to your house and packed them myself," Jacobs wrote back. "Mrs. S. was to nail the box up and send it to the RR this afternoon."

Swails's decision proved wise, as Democrats took pains to remind him that his life was in peril if he returned to South Carolina. "The white people," a *Kingstree Star* editorial affirmed in July 1879, "will not permit Swails to return here to live." If he ever even visited, he had to specify precisely when he would leave forever. "If he declines," the editorial warned, "he will have been aware of the fact that his residence here is at personal risk, and his permanently remaining here will not be tolerated by the whites of Williamsburg County. If after this he makes his appearance, he can take the consequences."*

---

*In December 1879, Swails sold his home in Kingstree. The sale, however, was apparently to a family friend and a ruse to protect Swails's wife and children, who continued living there. The property was conveyed back to Susan Swails in 1903. The home was torn down in the 1930s, and a tobacco warehouse was constructed on the site.

The Hampton administration also maintained its drumbeat of accusations against Swails, accusing him of corruption while presiding over the state senate. No charges were ever lodged, however, nor was any evidence of wrongdoing made public. Reviewing the many accusations, the *New York Times* found the government's inaction inconsistent with its claims. "In the County of Williamsburg," the *Times* noted, "ex-Senator Swails, a colored man of intelligence—a leader of his people—is accused of crimes almost innumerable, but the Democratic courts, with an apathy truly remarkable, do not attempt to indict, try, or punish him." If Swails were truly guilty of "robbery and the many other crimes charged against him," the newspaper asked, "why is he allowed to remain at large? Why is he not arrested by Democratic officers of the law? Why, in short, is he driven from the state in which it is alleged that he committed these crimes?"

As icing on the cake, Kelly of the Democratic Executive Committee, who had admitted Governor Hampton's complicity in the White Oak affair, sued Swails for libel, claiming that the former senator had fabricated his (Kelly's) statement. The court in Kingstree, which Democrats controlled, immediately seized Swails's home and property to satisfy any judgment. Fortunately, Swails's friend Sheriff Jacobs had authority over the home and property and refused to relinquish them unless a judgment actually issued. "His property is all in the hands of Sheriff Jacobs," the *Kingstree Star* complained, "by whose intervention alone it has been kept from being sold at public outcry long ago." Swails's attorney surmised that the threats against his client returning to Kingstree were motivated by the fact that Swails's time for responding to the libel suit had almost expired, offering Kelly an easy opportunity to seize the property. A newspaper in Maine following these events agreed. "Hearing that he was about to return," the paper concluded, "the published threat against his life was made to keep him away until judgment on the default could be taken against his property upon his failure to appear." In this instance, justice prevailed, and Kelly's complaint was dismissed.

Although now living in Washington, Swails maintained his Kingstree associations, commuting frequently by train. His family still lived there, and only three months after he left, Susan gave birth to a son, Stephen Jr. Little did she suspect that another of Swails's children, also named Stephen Jr., lived in New York.

Shortly before the 1880 elections, Swails decided to test the waters and paid a visit to Kingstree. Unable to stay away from politics, he gave a rousing speech at the local AME church that the local newspaper described as a "most bitter and diabolical race harangue." The *Newberry Herald* reported Swails "has returned to Williamsburg and is inaugurating measures for a vigorous campaign." According to the *Kingstree Star,* "It took us entirely by surprise, but with Swails to organize and hold communication with the greater lights at Washington and Sheriff Jacobs, who proposes to run for Sheriff again, as Lieutenant in Chief, we can undoubtedly look forward to as lively and live a campaign as Williamsburg can possibly get up. It will, most likely, if the radicals can organize, as we presume is Swails's purpose, be a desperate political encounter." The *Anderson Intelligencer,* expressing a theme picked up by other Democratic newspapers, surmised that Swails and his cohorts "have decided once again to lead the ignorant and duped colored men of South Carolina solidly for the overthrow of the conservative, wise and economic administration of the Democratic party, and for the re-establishment of that corrupt, ignorant and profligate reign which Republicans themselves have dubbed 'the era of good stealing.'"

Despite Swails's efforts, the 1880 election was another fiasco for the Republicans. Once again, the party did not run a candidate for governor, so Hampton's Democratic pick, the former Confederate general Johnson Hagood, won without opposition. With 142 Democrats and 6 Republicans elected to the General Assembly, the Democrats held an overwhelming majority in that body. Swails continued to visit Kingstree regularly, much to the Democrats' consternation, and newspapers tracked his comings and goings. Typical was an 1881 report in the *Yorkville Enquirer* announcing, "The notorious S. A. Swails is in Kingstree again."

As Swails soon discovered, the Democrats were up to their old tricks and had added a few new ones as well. Since 1880 was a census year, the legislature took advantage of the occasion to redraw the state's Seventh Congressional District to include most of the coastal areas, such as Beaufort, that contained large Black populations. While this ensured that the Seventh District would elect a Black representative, it also ensured that all the other districts would have white majorities and hence white representatives.

The practice of physical intimidation also continued under the term "bulldozing." An innovative method for rigging the outcome of elections, known as the "Eight Box Law," became increasingly popular as well. Passed by the legislature in 1882, this statute required separate ballot boxes for each position up for vote, such as state senator, congressman, and governor. Ballots placed in the incorrect box were disallowed. Because the name of the pertinent position appeared on each box, much of the Black voting population, which remained illiterate, was effectively disenfranchised. The law later required election managers to read the labels if a voter requested, but nothing ensured that they would read the labels correctly. Finally, the legislature enacted extremely restrictive voter-registration rules, which reduced the number of African Americans registered to vote in South Carolina from 58,000 in 1880 to fewer than 14,000 eight years later. Hampton and his successors had succeeded in ensuring white supremacy at the ballot box.

In 1884, Swails decided to run for Congress in the redrawn Seventh District. He technically qualified as a resident of Kingstree because he owned a home there, where his wife and children lived, even though he lived and worked outside of the state, which made him an "outsider" in the eyes of many. In February, he sent a letter to former congressman Rainey's brother "announcing his intention to canvas the 7th (or Black) District in his own interest as a candidate for Congressional honors," a local newspaper reported. As Williamsburg County was in the Seventh District, Swails believed he had a fighting chance. His chief competitor was Robert Smalls, a former slave who became a national celebrity during the Civil War when he stole a Confederate ship anchored in Charleston Harbor and turned it over to Union sailors blockading the harbor. He subsequently provided Union forces with valuable intelligence and championed the recruitment of Black soldiers. After the war, he became a prominent political figure in South Carolina, advancing programs meaningful to his African American constituency, serving in the General Assembly from 1868 through 1875 and in the US House of Representatives for several terms between 1875 and 1883.

On March 10, 1884, the Republicans met to select their Seventh District candidate. They decided on the first ballot, with Smalls receiving thirty-five votes, and Swails three votes. Although Smalls ran as the Republican candidate, the Democrats still viewed Swails as a threat. In 1886, as an act of revenge, South Carolina's two Democratic senators—former governor Hampton and Matthew C. Butler, another former

Confederate general—managed to get him fired from his post office job. "The reason given for his dismissal is that he is offensive to the South Carolina Democrats," a Washington newspaper reported. "In other words, he fought on the wrong side during the war." Swails, however, landed on his feet and procured a clerk's position in the Treasury Department's Office of the Auditor for the Post Office.

Although Swails did not run for office again, he remained involved in local politics and visited his family in Kingstree regularly. A trip there in September 1887 almost resulted in "a serious riot between the whites and blacks of that place owing to incendiary talk among the negroes by the notorious Radical politician Swails," according to the *Fairfield News and Herald*. "Eight wagons of armed negroes came into the town bent on a fight," the newspaper reported, "but the whites, by their coolness and determination, prevented a riot." In March 1888, Swails attended a Republican Executive Committee meeting in Columbia and, in May of that year, was selected as a delegate at large to the Republican National Convention in Chicago.

On behalf of the state's Republican Executive Committee, Swails in September 1888 wrote to South Carolina's governor, John P. Richardson. Election Day was approaching, he observed, and Democrats staffed all but one of the state's voting precincts, which he feared would make it difficult for Republicans to get a fair hearing. The solution, he advised the governor, required including a Republican representative at each precinct. Richardson declined his request, claiming that the state's election process was currently "the freest and fairest in the world" and that the corrupt Republican Party could not be trusted with oversight at the polls. "Those disgraceful scenes and unscrupulous manipulations of elections so confessedly prevalent during the days of Republican rule, are now, happily, things of the past, and can never return under the benignant way of Democratic principles, to curse and blast with horrors the peaceful, prosperous course of all the people of South Carolina," the governor asserted. In closing, Richardson noted, "your committee can scarcely be said to represent an organized party, as the comatose condition of the remnant of the Republicans in this State for many years past would surely justify the non-recognition of alleged rights and consequences so urgently demanded and strongly asserted by you."

In October 1888, Swails and other prominent Republicans held a four-hour rally in Sumter attended by some 2,000 Black citizens. The gathering was "the most enthusiastic that has been seen in the county for several years," a correspondent reported. The following year, Swails joined a delegation, along with Congressman Smalls, that met with the newly elected Republican president Benjamin Harrison to discuss governmental appointments. In 1890, he served as president of the South Carolina Republican Association. So far as can be determined, this was the last act of Stephen Swails's political career.

CHAPTER ELEVEN

A Proper Denouement to an Extraordinary Man

Throughout the 1880s and 1890s, Swails worked as a federal employee in Washington and continued practicing law in Kingstree. One of his more famous clients was Congressman Smalls. In 1886, Smalls's Democratic rival for the congressional seat was William Elliott, a white native of Beaufort County who had attended Harvard University, studied law at the University of Virginia, and served as a lieutenant in the Confederate army. Elliott pursued a successful law practice in Beaufort, where he was elected mayor and a member of the state house of representatives. Running for Congress in 1886, he defeated Smalls by 532 votes, even though the Seventh District was overwhelmingly Black and Republican.

Certain that the Democrats had resorted to their usual vote-rigging tactics, Smalls retained Swails to represent him and contested the election results before Congress's Committee on Elections. Smalls catalogued a litany of transgressions by Elliott and the Democrats, including the Board of County Canvassers' failure to list in the election returns all of the votes cast; the failure of poll managers at certain precincts to open the polls, to register qualified Black voters, and to deliberately commit irregularities to invalidate returns; and the practice of election managers to render fraudulent and illegal counts of ballots actually cast. In reply, Elliott denied Smalls's charges and countered that Smalls and his supporters had engaged in bribery, voter intimidation, and social ostracism of African American voters who desired to vote for Elliott but were fearful of doing so. He also contended that even though the Seventh District had a majority of Black voters, Smalls's conviction for taking bribes while a state senator had turned much of his constituency against him.*

---

*Smalls was convicted of bribery in 1877 by a jury composed of both races. He was pardoned in 1879 by Governor William D. Simpson as part of a general amnesty agreement.

For six days in early 1887, Swails took testimony from numerous witnesses and presented it to the committee. After reviewing the evidence, the committee's Democratic majority recommended that Elliott be seated as the Seventh District's duly elected representative, while the committee's Republican members predictably issued a minority report recommending that Smalls be awarded the seat. In early February 1889, the matter came up for debate in Congress and degenerated into rancorous squabbles among partisan factions. Cognizant that Democrats had a strong majority in the House, Republican members tried to appeal to their opponents' better natures. "Give this colored man, this former slave, this leader among his people, who has spent nearly all the earnings of his life since freedom contesting for the rights of which he has been cheated," a Republican urged. "Give to General Robert Smalls whose distinguished services for the Union and against rebellion, whose skills as a political organizer for his people and courage as a defender of the civil rights of his race early marked him for persecution and defamation." Despite the oratory, the final vote went along party lines in Elliott's favor, 147 to 142, with 33 members abstaining. Elliott was now the Seventh District's representative.

Over the years, Swails also renewed contact with members of the 54th Massachusetts. During the 1870s, many of the regiment's former officers, including Captains Appleton and Emilio, formed the Association of Officers of the 54th Massachusetts Volunteers. For several years, they attempted to locate Swails and finally, after writing his superiors in Washington, were able to reach him. The association's president, Lieutenant Colonel George Pope, wrote Swails:

Reports of your success in South Carolina before the Hampton administration have reached to all and for one I have been very proud that a Regimental comrade of mine has been able by his own exertions to put himself in the place occupied by you. At our meeting on the tenth last month, Col. W. P. Hallowell seconded by the 55th and 54th present invited me to prepare at our next meeting a paper on the Battle of Fort Wagner. Now, I can recollect very well my own impressions on that night. . . . So will you do me the favor of your leisure to give me such account as you can of your recollections of the affair, with also such as you remember of the deaths of Simpkins and Russel and also authentic as you can of the fight over the colors. . . . During your residence South, did you ever hear anything positive as to the deaths and burials of Cols. Shaw, Simpkins, Russel and Sergeant Simmons. I would like to make this paper I am to prepare as reliable as possible in all its accounts and details.

Swails's personal papers show that he responded to Pope's request and sent him a detailed recounting of the assault on Wagner and Captain Simpkins's last moments. He also received invitations to several of the association's gatherings, although how many he attended is unknown. The nature of the invitations, however, reflects the high regard in which his fellow officers held him. He also received requests for a photograph in uniform and information about the regiment, both from the association, which was preparing a history of the 54th Massachusetts, and from Joseph T. Wilson, who was compiling a roster of the African American regiments. "In complying with this request," Wilson wrote, "you will aid the Post in preserving the memory of the struggle for Freedom, as well as the heroism of thousands of comrades that else must be lost to the coming generations."

Perhaps the most telling letter that Swails received is from May 1897, inviting him to attend the dedication in Boston of a monument to Colonel Shaw. "I am requested by Colonel N. P. Hallowell, who will command a battalion of survivors of the 54th and 55th regiments infantry and the 5th Massachusetts Cavalry, to further invite you to be present at the dedication of the Col. Shaw Memorial on May 31 and to extend to you an invitation to ride on his personal staff on that occasion." A photograph taken during the ceremony reveals that Swails did indeed attend this event, marching a short distance behind William Carney, who carried the tattered American flag that he had rescued during the assault on Fort Wagner. His participation in the parade and the invitation to ride with Colonel Hallowell's personal staff demonstrates Swails's exalted standing among his fellow veterans.

Ill health plagued Swails's final days. On February 16, 1899, he entered a private sanatorium "for surgery and rest cure" in Washington, where he received treatment for three weeks. He left the facility on March 9, and the next day, his superior at the Treasury Department, Henry A. Cauth, wrote Swails's son, Florian, that his father was "in very bad shape, mentally and physically." Swails had been a "very efficient, faithful clerk," Cauth assured him, "and we all deeply regret his misfortune." Cauth explained that the department could pay a disabled employee such as Swails for sixty days, but after that, he would be on his own. Florian offered to serve in his father's stead, but Cauth responded that the department could not accept his proposal.

Apparently, Swails returned to Kingstree to convalesce, and his medical condition improved over the ensuing weeks. On April 1, 1899, George A. Cooper of the Treasury Department wrote Swails that he was "so glad to hear you were improving so fast. You must take it easy," he advised, "and build up all you can while you have a chance at the fresh air of the country." That same day, another Treasury official wrote him that "news of your recovery and the probability that you will be with us again is indeed most gratifying to me. Scarcely a day passes," he continued, "during which your name is not mentioned by some of your former fellow clerks, the earnestness of whose solicitations make me know that they all are anxious to see you back again."

Swails's condition, however, took a turn for the worse during the following year. On May 12, 1900, his temperature rose to 102 degrees, and he suffered from "acute dysentery." Dr. D. C. Scott, who cared for him, reported that Swails "developed symptoms of congestion of the brain [and] rapidly became worse" on May 17, 1900, "and died in 5 or 6 hours in a comatose condition." Swails was sixty-eight years of age.

On May 24, the *Williamsburg County Record* published Swails's obituary on its front page. This was the first time the newspaper had ever published a Black citizen's obituary.

S. A. Swails, who figured so prominently in the history of this county during the days of Reconstruction, died at his home in this place on Thursday of last week. His health had been failing for some time and his death, although rather sudden, was not altogether unexpected.

Swails was born in the State of New York, but settled in Kingstree directly after the civil war, and took a prominent part in establishing Republican rule in this county.

He was elected to the state senate a number of terms and was at one time mayor of Kingstree.

After the Democrats succeeded in wrestling the reigns [*sic*] of government from the Republican party, Swails went to Washington and secured a position in the Department of the Interior [*sic*], which he held until a few months ago, when he was forced by failing health to resign. He returned to his home in Kingstree where he spent the balance of his days.

Susan buried her husband's body in Charleston's Humane and Friendly Society Cemetery. Free Blacks had established the society in the early 1800s to assist Black families and provide burial plots for African Americans, who were forbidden burial in the same cemeteries as whites. In 1843, the society acquired burial grounds adjacent to Magnolia Cemetery, where the remains of many prominent white Charlestonians—including some 1,700 Confederate soldiers—were buried. It is not clear why Susan chose to inter Swails in Charleston rather than Kingstree, although one commentator later suggested she might have selected the city out of concern that his former political opponents back home would desecrate his grave if she buried him there.

What of Swails's survivors? There is no evidence that he ever contacted Sarah or their two children, Stephen Jr. and Minnie, after his marriage to Susan Aspinall in 1866. Indeed, according to Susan, he never mentioned his former liaison and offspring to her. As for Susan, she continued living in Kingstree, where she passed away a few years after her husband's death. Their older son, Florian, married in 1897, raised a large family, and lived in Kingstree until his death in 1935. The couple's other son, Stephen Jr., was married in Charleston and lived there until dying in 1939.

The public's perception of Stephen Swails has evolved dramatically since his death. Four years after his demise, Samuel D. McGill published his *Narrative of Reminiscences in Williamsburg County*. McGill, who had personally experienced Reconstruction in Williamsburg County, reported that violence there had been mild compared to elsewhere in South Carolina. He observed, "S. A. Swails, a colored soldier in a Pennsylvania [*sic*] Union Regiment, was a state senator and possessed unbounded influence over the Negroes and to him it is principally due the exemption as above, and there was no serious complaints against him."

In 1923, William Willis Bodie, in his *History of Williamsburg County*, adopted an attitude reminiscence of the attacks leveled by Democrats while Swails was still alive. "There came out of Potter's Raiders to Williamsburg a Pennsylvania Negro named Stephen A. Swails," he wrote. "It was not then known that he had been one of this band, but often suspected. Had it been known, the first one of at least of a hundred men in Williamsburg who saw him would have shot him like a snake." Bodie conceded that Swails "was an educated Negro and had much natural ability," exercising "an uncanny influence over the Negroes" and serving as the county's senator "until he was driven away by outraged whites." In 1936, county historian Henry E. Davis adopted a similar tone, delivering an address in which he boasted that Captain William M. Kinder had "led a successful movement for the expulsion from the community of the notorious mulatto lawyer from Pennsylvania, S. A. Swails, who had settled here after serving his apprenticeship in rascality as a colonel in Potter's raid."

More recently, Swails has begun to receive the recognition and praise due to him. Kingstree attorney William "Billy" Jenkinson undertook a thorough study of the man and spearheaded a drive to place a historical marker on the site of Swails's former residence at the corner of East Main and North Brooks Streets. Through Jenkinson's efforts, the Williamsburg Historical Society sponsored the marker's dedication on May 30, 1998, complete with an appearance by 54th Massachusetts Regiment reenactors headed by Joseph McGill, a noted African American historian and Kingstree native, and a speech by Congressman James Clyburn. The plaque states that Swails lived in a house on the site and describes his accomplishments, including his service with the 54th Massachusetts, his work with the Freedmen's Bureau, his law practice, his tenures in the state senate and as Kingstree's intendant, and his work as editor of the *Williamsburg Republican*.

In October 2006, the African American Historical Alliance, cochaired by Jenkinson and Jannie Hariot and boasting a membership of several prominent historians, organized a ceremony to erect a monument at Swails's grave and to hold a commemoration of his life. The gravesite was unmarked at the time, but Russell Horres, a board member of the alliance, discovered an old map of the Humane and Friendly Society Cemetery that identified the grave's location. Several of Swails's descendants, cadets from The Citadel, Black Civil War reenactors, and a sizeable audience of Black and white participants attended the ceremony. A five-foot-tall blue-granite monument was placed at his gravesite, a band played, and a cannon fired a salute, capping an event described by a Kingstree newspaper as a "proper denouement to an extraordinary man who faced battles and bigotry to become an American hero."

In 2008, in recognition of Swails's six-year tenure as the first Black president pro tempore of the South Carolina Senate, state senators proclaimed that Swails's many contributions "to the wellbeing of the citizens of South Carolina and his struggles for equality among individuals are numerous and greatly deserving of permanent recognition and tribute in a place of honor in the Senate Chamber where he served with such great distinction." Accordingly, they issued a resolution authorizing Swails's portrait to be hung in the senate chamber, joining those of other distinguished senators. The African American Historical Alliance commissioned Michael Del Priore, who had made six portraits already displayed in the senate and house chambers, to paint Swails's portrait, which he completed and presented to the senate. A change in senate leadership intervened, however, and as of 2021, the portrait had yet to be hung.

Fittingly, a recent scholarly study of the three Black Massachusetts regiments—the 54th and 55th Infantry and the 5th Cavalry—gives Swails his just due. "No veteran of the three black regiments reached the political heights achieved by Lieutenant Stephen A. Swails," writes Douglas R. Egerton. "Nor did any of the other tens of thousands of black men who had served during the Civil War."

Epilogue

Stephen Swails made significant contributions to the advancement of the nation's African American citizens. He volunteered for service in the premier Black regiment raised in the North, fully aware of the risks of combat and of the draconian treatment the Confederacy promised captured Black soldiers. Colonel Hallowell justly gave Swails "special praise for his coolness, bravery, and efficiency," describing his conduct in battle as exemplary. The 54th Massachusetts's sterling performance under fire dispelled concerns over whether African American troops could fight on par with whites and helped pave the way for the acceptance of some 200,000 Black soldiers in the Union armed forces. His was a prominent voice in demanding the same pay for Black soldiers as whites received, a point on which he and his companions ultimately prevailed. And he fought tenaciously for the right to advancement as a commissioned officer, an honor denied him because of his "African Blood." He won that fight as well.

Despite the efforts of Swails and men like him, prejudice against African Americans persisted in the military. Black officers could not command white troops, and senior officers remained invariably white. Black regiments fought in the Indian Wars and the Spanish-American War. During World War I, 386,000 African Americans served in segregated regiments led by white officers. Still, none held positions commanding whites. During World War II, African Americans constituted close to 10 percent of the army's enlisted ranks, but the outfits remained segregated, and the policy of assigning white officers to Black units persisted. After the war, the military opened the way for more African Americans to become commissioned officers, and racial segregation in the army finally ended during the Korean War, when the military addressed troop shortages by assigning Black soldiers to white regiments. In 1951, to bring order into this process, the army initiated a quota system, limiting the percentage of African Americans permitted in a unit. This was abolished shortly before the Vietnam War, during which most of the impediments that Blacks had formerly faced were removed.

During the Persian Gulf War in 1990, Chairman of the Joint Chiefs of Staff General Colin L. Powell, an African American, lead the US military effort. In 1997, General Powell spoke in Boston at a ceremony rededicating the monument to Colonel Shaw and the 54th Massachusetts. Before the Civil War had ended, Powell noted, some 200,000 African Americans had served in the military. "As a result of their service, they had helped preserve the Union and moved us one step closer to equality," he continued. "But even with the 13th and 14th and 15th Amendments, we still didn't get all the blessings of liberty or what had been earned by the service of black men." The cumulative efforts of those who came before him, however, had brought considerable progress. "I stand before you as a direct descendant of every one of those Negroes," Powell asserted. "I was able to rise to become chairman of the Joint Chiefs of Staff, the senior military position in the armed forces of the United States, but I have a direct lineage back to the men of the 54th."

Swails failed to achieve full equality for Black soldiers, but his efforts were significant milestones in the process that ultimately approached that end. He also devoted much of his life attempting to secure Black parity with whites in the political and social spheres, but white supremacy exerted too powerful a hold on the South for him to succeed in that arena. Reconstruction in South Carolina sputtered to a close in 1877 with the recognition of Hampton as governor and Hayes's presidential compromise with the Democrats. The ensuing years witnessed Black voters' virtual disenfranchisement and the termination of most Reconstruction measures aimed at fostering racial equality. White supremacy remained the battle cry of the "Redeemers," culminating in 1879 in a law prohibiting interracial marriage. Other reforms, such as revitalizing the public-school system, ran aground from a lack of funds. In 1880, more than three-quarters of South Carolina's Black population was illiterate.

The situation for the state's African Americans deteriorated further in 1890 with "Pitchfork" Ben Tillman's election as governor. In his inaugural address, Tillman used familiar language to describe his electoral victory as the "triumph of democracy and white supremacy over mongrelism and anarchy, of civilization over barbarism." Whites, he proclaimed, now exercised "absolute control" over the state government and were determined "at any all hazards to retain it."

Due largely to Tillman's efforts, a convention in 1895 drafted a new state constitution, with the goal of completing the disenfranchisement of Blacks. As Tillman, who was now a US senator, announced, Southerners "have never recognized the right of the negro to govern white men, and we never will." The resulting constitution, which defined a Black person as someone having "one eighth or more negro blood," went far toward achieving that goal, requiring Black and white children to attend separate schools and forbidding interracial marriage. While the US Constitution prohibited states from passing laws disenfranchising Black citizens, the new South Carolina Constitution effectively did just that. To vote, a citizen now had to pass a literacy test, own property worth at least $300, and pay a poll tax.

The following year, the US Supreme Court, in *Plessy v. Ferguson,* approved racial segregation by permitting "separate" accommodations and facilities so long as they were "equal." Subsequent legislation required segregation in streetcars, trolleys, railroad coaches, and textile mills, while signs proclaiming "White only" and "Colored only" governed the use of water fountains, waiting rooms, restrooms, hotel rooms, and other public accommodations. "Jim Crow" legislation of the 1890s and into the twentieth century completed the process of ensuring racial segregation and disenfranchising African Americans in the South.

Not until the civil rights advances of the mid-twentieth century did some of Reconstruction's promises approach fulfillment. To the extent modern advocates of racial equality and the advancement of African Americans have achieved success, it is because they have, as the saying goes, stood on the shoulders of giants.

Stephen Atkins Swails was one of those giants.

CITATIONS FOR QUOTATIONS

CHAPTER ONE
An Angel of God Come Down to Lead the Host of Freedom

2   "own imprudence": *Columbia (PA) Spy,* August 23, 1834.

2   "the practice of others in employing the negroes": Ibid., August 30, 1834.

3   "there must be an underground railroad somewhere": Edmond Raymond Turner, "The Underground Railroad in Pennsylvania," *Pennsylvania Magazine of History and Biography* 36, no. 3 (1912): 312.

3   "devise some means to prevent the further influx": William Frederic Worner, "The Columbia Race Riots of 1834 and 1835," in *Historical Papers and Addresses of the Lancaster County Historical Society,* vol. 26 (Lancaster, 1922), 180.

3   "at a reduced price": *Columbia (PA) Spy,* September 3, 1834.

4   "lying in his own blood amidst the rubble": Thomas P. Slaughter, *Bloody Dawn: The Christiana Riot and Racial Violence in the Antebellum North* (New York: Oxford University Press, 1991), 176.

4   "reflected from the walls of the neighboring houses": *Columbia (PA) Spy,* October 4, 1834.

4   "not agreeable and the less you appear": Ibid., March 7, 1835.

6   "one of those mean, cunning, drunken, thieving 'niggers'": Articles reproduced in "Kinder and Gentler: An Exchange between Two Cooperstown, N.Y., Weeklies, 1868," *New York History,* 71, no. 3 (July 1992): 375–80.

7   "whether the enterprise of John Brown and his associates": Henry Greenleaf Pearson, *The Life of John A. Andrew,* 2 vols. (Boston: Houghton Mifflin, 1904), 1:100.

7   "such corps of infantry for the volunteer military service": US War Department, *The War of the Rebellion: A Compilation of Official Records of the Union and Confederate Armies,* 130 vols. (Washington, DC: Government Printing Office, 1880–1901), ser. 3, 3:20. Cited hereafter as *OR.* Unless otherwise indicated, all *OR* citations are to series 1.

7   "success or failure": Andrew to Shaw, January 30, 1863, in Pearson, *Life of John Andrew,* 74–75.

8   "His bearing was graceful": Lewis F. Emilio, *A Brave Black Regiment: History of the Fifty-Fourth Regiment of Massachusetts Volunteer Infantry 1863–1865* (Boston: Boston Book, 1894), 5.

8   "the more ardent, faithful, and true Republicans": Andrew to Francis Shaw, January 30, 1863, ibid., 4.

8   "Please destroy my letter and telegraph": Robert Shaw to Francis Shaw, February 5, 1863, in Peter Burchard, *One Gallant Rush: Robert Gould Shaw and His Brave Black Regiment* (New York: St. Martin's, 1965), 74.

8   "convinced I shall never regret having taken this step": Robert Shaw to Annie, February 8, 1863, in *Blue-Eyed Child of Fortune: The Civil War Letters of Colonel Robert Gould Shaw,* ed. Russell Duncan (Athens: University of Georgia Press, 1992), 286.

8   "a gallant and fine fellow": Emilio, *Brave Black Regiment,* 4.

9   "If you cannot have a whole loaf": Duncan, *Blue-Eyed Child of Fortune,* 26.

9   "TO COLORED MEN!": Ibid., 27.

9   "Colored Men to prove their Manhood and Loyalty": Ibid., 27.

9   "When first the rebel cannon shattered": Frederick Douglass, "Men of Color, to Arms!" *Douglass Monthly,* March 21, 1863. See also Dudley Taylor Cornish, *The Sable Arm* (Lawrence: University Press of Kansas, 1956), 108–9.

9   "first to break the chains of her slaves": Burchard, *One Gallant Rush,* 79.

10   "Public opinion in the North was either avowedly hostile": Norwood Penrose Hallowell, *The Negro as a Soldier in the War of the Rebellion* (Boston: Little, Brown, 1897), 6.

10   "prove that a Negro can be made a good soldier": Shaw to Annie, February 8, 1863, in Duncan, *Blue-Eyed Child of Fortune,* 285.

10   "Our people must know that if they are ever to attain": James Henry Gooding to Editor, March 3, 1863, in *On the Altar of Freedom: A Black Soldier's Civil War Letters from the Front,* ed. Virginia M. Adams (Amherst: University of Massachusetts Press, 1991), 4.

11   "quite wonderful": Hallowell, *Negro as a Soldier,* 9.

11   "not exaggerate when I say that there is no regiment superior": George E. Stephens to Editor, May 1, 1863, in *A Voice of Thunder: A Black Soldier's Civil War,* ed. Donald Yacovone (Urbana: University of Illinois Press, 1998), 235.

11   "rather an uncommon amount of muscle": *Springfield (MA) Republican,* n.d., quoted in Duncan, *Blue-Eyed Child of Fortune,* 36.

12   "a tip-top man": J. M. Forbes to Andrew, February 2, 1863, quoted in Duncan, *Blue-Eyed Child of Fortune,* 28.

12   "Vast crowds lined the streets": Emilio, *Brave Black Regiment,* 33.

12   "never forget the scene": Burchard, *One Gallant Rush,* 94.

13   "No scouts need ever to be sent out": *Boston Pilot,* n.d., quoted in Duncan, *Blue-Eyed Child of Fortune,* 40.

13   "the sun sank into the sea": Emilio, *Brave Black Regiment,* 35.

CHAPTER TWO

One Plane of Ashes and Blackened Chimneys

14   "from the appearance of the men": Hunter to Andrew, June 3, 1863, *OR,* 14:462–63.

14   "Our reception was almost as enthusiastic here": Gooding to Editors, June 8, 1863, in Adams, *On the Altar of Freedom*, 26.

15   "impossible to keep clean here": Shaw to father, June 6, 1863, in Duncan, *Blue-Eyed Child of Fortune*, 339–40.

15   "beat the enemy whenever and wherever": Edward A. Miller, *Lincoln's Abolitionist General: The Biography of David Hunter* (Columbia: University of South Carolina Press, 1997), 96.

17   "keen gray eyes, a long nose": Theodore Clarke Smith, *The Life and Letters of James Abram Garfield*, 2 vols. (New Haven, CT: Yale University Press, 1925), 1:127.

17   "It is time slavery had its quietus": Miller, *Lincoln's Abolitionist General*, 79.

17   "authority to arm such loyal men": Hunter to Stanton, April 3, 1862, *OR*, 6:263–64.

17   "to send immediately to these headquarters": Smith to Benham, May 9, 1862, ibid., ser. 3, 2:31.

17   "never, in my judgment": Phillips to Pierce, May 13, 1862, ibid., 59–60.

18   "neither General Hunter, nor any other commander": Abraham Lincoln, *Speeches and Writings, 1859–1865* (New York: Library of America, 1989), 318–19.

18   "This conscription, together with the manner of its execution": Wells to Pierce, *OR*, ser. 3, 2:58–59.

18   "The President argued that the nation": New York Times, August 6, 1862.

18   "arm, equip, and receive into service": Stanton to Saxton, August 25, 1862, *OR*, 14:377–78.

18   "It is admitted on all hands that the negroes fought": Saxton's Report, November 12, 1862, ibid., 189–90.

19   "It is my belief that scarcely an incident in this war": Saxton's Report, March 14, 1864, ibid., 226.

19   "splendid, but impulsive and changeable": Higginson's War Journal, March 24, 1864, in *The Complete Civil War Journal and Selected Letters of Thomas Wentworth Higginson*, ed. Christopher Looby (Chicago: University of Chicago Press, 2000), 116.

19   "allows no swearing or drinking": Shaw to mother, June 6, 1863, in Duncan, *Blue-Eyed Child of Fortune*, 339.

20   "For sound sense and real native eloquence": *Boston Commonwealth*, July 10, 1863.

20   "Our colored troops are more than a match": *New York Times*, February 10, 1863.

20   "in every action the negro troops have behaved": Saxton to Stanton, March 14, 1864, *OR*, 14:226.

20   "as efficient a regiment I believe as there is": Stephen R. Wise, *Gate of Hell: Campaign for Charleston Harbor, 1863* (Columbia: University of South Carolina Press, 1994), 47.

21   "is but the initial step of a system": Hunter to Andrew, June 3, 1863, *OR*, 14:462–63.

21   "Colonel Montgomery with his forces": Hunter to Stanton, June 3, 1864, ibid., 463.

21   "inaugurate a servile war": General Order No. 60, Richmond, August 21, 1862,
      ibid., 599.

21   "not entitled to be considered as soldiers": General Order No. 111, Richmond,
      December 24, 1862, ibid., ser. 2, 5:795–97.

21   "every white person being a commissioned officer": Joint Resolutions adopted
      by the Confederate Congress on the Subject of Retaliation, May 1, 1863, ibid.,
      940–41.

21   "You say you are fighting for liberty": Hunter to Davis, April 23, 1863, *OR*, 14:448–
      49. Whether Davis received Hunter's letter is not known.

22   "good man to begin under": Shaw to father, June 5, 1863, in Duncan, *Blue-Eyed
      Child of Fortune*, 339.

22   "the justice or generosity of your judgment": Hunter to Montgomery, June 9,
      1863, ibid., 466–67.

23   "a small craft that looked like a canal boat": Emilio, *Brave Black Regiment*, 39.

23   "The foliage is wonderfully thick": Shaw to Annie, June 9, 1863, in Duncan, *Blue-
      Eyed Child of Fortune*, 341.

23   "How soon can you be ready": Ibid., 342.

23   "On the way up, Montgomery threw several shells": Ibid.

24   "Going through the house": John W. M. Appleton Letter Journal, John W. M.
      Appleton Papers, West Virginia and Regional History Center, Morristown, 20.

24   "thoroughly disemboweled": in Duncan, *Blue-Eyed Child of Fortune*, 342–43.

25   "The riverbank was a sheet of flame": Emilio, *Brave Black Regiment*, 43.

25   "one plane of ashes and of Blackened chimneys": *Savannah Daily Morning News*,
      June 16, 1863, quoted in Spencer B. King Jr., *Darien: The Death and Rebirth of a
      Southern Town* (Macon, GA: Mercer University Press, 1981), 71.

25   "Besides my own distaste for this barbarous sort of warfare": Shaw to Annie,
      June 9, 1863, in Duncan, *Blue-Eyed Child of Fortune*, 343.

25   "I think now, as I did at the time": Ibid., 360–61.

26   "for no reasons which convey any imputation": Lincoln to Hunter, June 30, 1863,
      quoted in Miller, *Lincoln's Abolitionist General*, 154–55.

26   "everyone likes and admires Gen. Gillmore": Looby, *Complete Civil War Journal
      and Selected Letters of Thomas Wentworth Higginson*, 157.

26   "brilliant young officer who had recently arrived": Emilio, *Brave Black Regiment*, 46.

27   "I was the more disappointed at being left behind": Shaw to Strong, July 6, 1863,
      in Buchard, *One Gallant Rush*, 117–18.

CHAPTER THREE

Looking Out from among the Ghastly Corpses

29   "The James Island line is their best": Beauregard to J. H. Trapier, April 5, 1863,
      OR, 14:880–81.

29   "the strongest single earthwork": Emilio, *Brave Black Regiment*, 70.

32   "We have not had our clothes off since we left": Shaw to Annie, July 13, 1863, in Duncan, *Blue-Eyed Child of Fortune,* 381.

32   "much hard thinking": Emilio, *Brave Black Regiment,* 56.

33   "That was something the rebels didn't expect": Gooding to Editors, July 20, 1863, in Adams, *On the Altar of Freedom,* 37.

33   "boys of the Tenth Connecticut could not help loving": Article from *The Reflector,* reproduced in Emilio, *Brave Black Regiment,* 60.

34   "all bearing evidence of struggles with bush and brier": Ibid.

34   "the steadiness and soldierly conduct": Alfred H. Terry's Report, July 16, 1863, *OR,* 28(1):755.

34   "It is not for us to blow our horn": Gooding to Editor, July 20, 1863, in Adams, *On the Altar of Freedom,* 38.

34   "For the first time colored men had been hand to hand": John M. W. Appleton, "That Night at Fort Wagner; by One Who Was There," *Putnam's Magazine* 4, no. 19 (July, 1869): 10–11.

34   "very gratifying to us personally": Shaw to Annie, July 15, 1863, in Duncan, *Blue-Eyed Child of Fortune,* 385.

35   "For nearly half a mile we had to pass over a bridge": Shaw to Annie, July 17, 1863, ibid., 386.

35   "groping their way and grasping their leaders": Emilio, *Brave Black Regiment,* 64–65.

35   "for the lightning to show us our way": Appleton, "That Night at Fort Wagner," 11.

35   "I never had such an extraordinary walk": Shaw to Annie, July 17, 1863, in Duncan, *Blue-Eyed Child of Fortune,* 386.

36   "Well done!" Emilio, *Brave Black Regiment,* 67.

36   "Words cannot depict the thunder": Brian C. Pohanka, "Fort Wagner and the 54th Massachusetts Volunteer Infantry," *America's Civil War* (September 1991), available online at https://www.battlefields.org/learn/articles/fort-wagner-and-54th-massachusetts-volunteer-infantry.

36   "We are all going into Wagner like a flock of sheep": Burchard, *One Gallant Rush,* 133.

36   "Well I guess we will let Strong lead": Testimony of Nathaniel Paige, *New York Tribune,* before the American Freedman's Inquiry Commission, February 1864, quoted in Wise, *Gate of Hell,* 100.

36   "Fifty-fourth Massachusetts, a colored regiment": Seymour's Report, November 10, 1863, *OR,* 28(1):347.

37   "it was believed that the Fifty-fourth": Emilio, *Brave Black Regiment,* 75.

37   "You may lead the column": Ibid., 72.

38   "All was ominous of the impending onslaught": Ibid., 72–76.

38   "low tones with each other": Appleton Letter Journal, Appleton Papers, 46.

38   "Don't fire a musket on the way up": Emilio, *Brave Black Regiment,* 77.

39   "Attention!": Ibid., 79.

39   "cheering as if going on some mirthful errand": Stephens to Editor, July 21, 1863, in Yacovone, *Voice of Thunder,* 245.

39   "The center only had a free path": Emilio, *Brave Black Regiment,* 80.

39   "with set jaws": Ibid.

39   "It was the calm that precedes the reloading": Garth W. James, "The Assault on Fort Wagner," in *Papers Read before the Commandery of the State of Wisconsin, Military Order of the Loyal Legion of the United States,* vol. 1 (Milwaukee: Burdick, Armitage, and Allen, 1891), 23.

39   "Exposed to the direct fire of canister and musketry": Hallowell's Report, November 7, 1863, *OR,* 28(1):362.

39   "Forward, Fifty-fourth!": Emilio, *Brave Black Regiment,* 79.

39   "The garrison fought with muskets": Ibid., 82.

40   "It would have been impossible": Swails, "Statement of S. A. Swails 1st Sergeant Co. F. 54th Regt. Mass. Vols. Made to Henry W. Littlefield, August 12, 1863," Stephen A. Swails Personal Papers, copies in William "Billy" Jenkinson Personal Collection, Kingstree, SC (hereafter Swails Personal Papers).

41   "The genius of Dante": Elbridge J. Copp, *Reminiscences of the War of the Rebellion 1861–1865* (Nashua, NH: Telegraph, 1911), 242.

41   "And then we saw the lightning": Harriet Tubman, quoted in Kate Larson, *Bound for the Promised Land: Harriet Tubman, Portrait of an American Hero* (New York: One World, Ballantine Books, 2004), 220.

41   "a painful and unnecessary interval": Seymour's Report, November 10, 1863, *OR,* 28(1):347.

41   "what had been so dearly bought": Ibid., 348.

42   "imbibed rather freely": Stephens to Editor, August 8, 1863, in Yacovone, *Voice of Thunder,* 246.

42   "You know how much harder they will fare": Emilio, *Brave Black Regiment,* 103.

42   "blood, mud, water, brains": Robert C. Gilchrist, "Confederate Defense of Morris Island," in *Charleston Yearbook, 1884* (Charleston, SC: News and Courier, 1884), 370.

43   "probably no battlefield in the country": *Charleston Courier,* July 21, 1863.

43   "Overconfidence, poor preparation, too much space and time": Wise, *Gate of Hell,* 118.

43   "I saw them fight at Wagner as none but splendid soldiers": *New York Herald,* July 19, 1863.

43   "The negroes fought gallantly": Iredell Jones, quoted in Emilio, *Brave Black Regiment,* 95.

43   "made Fort Wagner such a name for the colored race": *New York Tribune,* reproduced in Douglas R. Egerton, *Thunder at the Gates* (New York: Basic Books, 2016), 142.

43   "The thousand little sand-hills": Clara Barton, quoted in Isabel Ross, *Angel of the Battlefield* (New York: Harper and Brothers, 1956), 66.

43   "mourn over our own loss and that of the regiment": Francis Shaw to Dr. Lincoln Stone, August 3, 1863, in Duncan, *Blue-Eyed Child of Fortune,* 54.

44   "We hold that a soldier's most appropriate burial-place": Francis Shaw to Gillmore, August 24, 1863, in Emilio, *Brave Black Regiment,* 102–3.

CHAPTER FOUR
Why Can't We Have a Soldier's Pay?

45 "was the saddest in the history of the Fifty-fourth": Emilio, *Brave Black Regiment*, 105.

45 "The faces and forms of all showed plainly": Ibid., 111.

46 "Few men are more capable of active": Stephens to editor, September 4, 1863, in Yacavone, *Voice of Thunder*, 260.

46 "sixteen hours in twenty-four in the midst of fire": Clara Barton, quoted in Wise, *Gate of Hell*, 187.

46 "the little sand flies with white mugs": Charles B. Bowditch, "War Letters of Charles B. Bowditch," *Proceedings of the Massachusetts Historical Society*, 3rd ser., vol. 57 (Boston: Massachusetts Historical Society, 1924), 429.

47 "special duty in the trenches": "Major Brooks' Journal of Engineer Operations Executed Under His Direction on Morris Island, Between July 12 and September 7, 1863," *OR*, 28(1):298 (August 31, 1863).

48 "It is a duty of the greatest danger": Stephens to Editor, September 4, 1863, in Yacovone, *Voice of Thunder*, 260.

48 "Up and down through the trenches and the parallels": Emilio, *Brave Black Regiment*, 123.

48 "in no military operations of the war": Brooks, "Colored Troops for Work," September 10, 1863, *OR*, 28(1):328.

48 "wrested from the enemy by your persevering courage and skill": Gillmore, General Congratulatory Order, September 15, 1863, *OR*, 28:40.

49 "I must say that while the agreement and harmony": Bowditch, "War Letters," 444.

49 "The startling news of the mobs": Stephens to Editor, August 7, 1863, in Yacovone, *Voice of Thunder*, 250.

50 "Too many of our comrades' bones": Gooding to Editor, August 9, 1863, in Adams, *On the Altar of Freedom*, 49.

50 "The paymaster is here to pay you": Stephens to Thomas Hamilton, October 3, 1863, in Yacovone, *Voice of Thunder*, 61.

51 "fell with crushing outcome": Ibid.

51 "Why can't we have a soldiers pay?": Gooding to President Lincoln, September 28, 1863, in Adams, *On the Altar of Freedom*, 119–20.

51 "to the world as holding out": Emilio, *Brave Black Regiment*, 137.

51 "Since [April 1863] I have performed": Swails, quoted in Ira Berlin et al., "Writing Freedom's History," *Prologue* 14, no. 3 (Fall 1982): 137–38.

52 "think of what the men do and suffer": Emilio, *Brave Black Regiment*, 79.

52 "Now it seems strange to me": Edward D. Washington letter, March 13, 1864, in *A Grand Army of Black Men: Letters from African American Soldiers in the Union Army, 1861–1865*, ed. Edwin S. Redkey (New York: Cambridge University Press, 1992), 46.

53 "the law of nations": President Lincoln's Proclamation, reproduced in Emilio, *Brave Black Regiment*, 96–97.

53 "uncivilized use": *Charleston Mercury*, August 13, 1863.

53 "All of you can now rejoice": Wise, *Gate of Hell*, 127.

54 "First, to procure an outlet for cotton": Gillmore to H. W. Halleck, January 31, 1864, *OR*, 35(1):279.

55 "No more fatigue at the front!": Emilio, *Brave Black Regiment*, 148.

55 "All enjoyed the change of landscape": Ibid., 149.

CHAPTER FIVE

I Now Recommend His Being Allowed to Serve as a Commissioned Officer

56 "take his men and catch the rebels": Emilio, *Brave Black Regiment*, 152.

56 "In general appearance": Rufus S. Jones, March 20, 1864, in Redkey, *Grand Army of Black Men*, 40.

58 "neither general had much faith in the success": Capt. Gustavas Sullivan Dana quoted in William H. Nulty, *Confederate Florida: The Road to Olustee* (Tuscaloosa: University of Alabama Press, 1990), 101.

58 "By the time you receive this": Patrick Egan, *The Florida Campaign with Light Battery C, Third Rhode Island Heavy Artillery, Personal Narrative of Events in the War of the Rebellion, Being Papers Read before the Rhode Island Soldiers and Sailors Historical Society* (Wilmington, NC: Broadfoot, 1993), 482.

58 "very unsteady and queer": John Hay quoted in Tyler Dennett, ed., *Lincoln and the Civil War in the Diaries and Letters of John Hay* (New York: Dodd, Meade, 1939), 164.

59 "We're bound for Tallahassee": Emilio, *Brave Black Regiment*, 159.

59 "That's home-made thunder": Ibid., 162.

60 "We're badly whipped": Ibid., 163.

60 "Its thrilling notes": Robert P. Broadwater, *The Battle of Olustee, 1864: The Final Union Attempt to Seize Florida* (Jefferson, NC: McFarland, 1958), 121.

60 "go in and save the corps": *Chicago Tribune*, March 9, 1864, quoted in Broadwater, *Battle of Olustee*, 132.

61 "Shooting niggers": Noah Andre Trudeau, *Like Men of War: Black Troops in the Civil War, 1862–1865* (Boston: Little, Brown, 1998), 151.

61 "We will hang every damned negro officer we catch": Stephens to Editor, March 10, 1864, in Redkey, *Grand Army of Black Men*, 46.

61 "never forget the cry": Joseph H. Walker letter, May 14, 1864, ibid., 54.

61 "do not seem to understand anything": Rufus letter, May 17, 1864, ibid., 54–55.

61 "The narrow road was choked": Emilio, *Brave Black Regiment*, 170.

62 "did what ought to insure": Dr. Marsh quoted in Emilio, *Brave Black Regiment*, 174–75.

62 "We have had a fight": *Chicago Tribune*, March 9, 1864, quoted in Cornish, *Sable Arm*, 268.

62 "There seems to have been a strange ignorance": Stephens to Editor, March 10, 1864, in Redkey, *Grand Army of Black Men*, 45.

62 "behaved creditably": Seymour's Report, March 25, 1864, *OR*, 35(1):290.

62 "There is much feeling about it": Higginson to Louisa, February 23, 1864, in Looby, *Complete Civil War Journal and Selected Letters of Thomas Wentworth Higginson*, 356.

63 "Sergeant Stephen A. Swails, acting sergeant-major": Hallowell's Report, March 1, 1864, *OR*, 35(1):315.

63 "darker than most officers": Commission signed by Governor Andrew, March 11, 1864; Emilio, *Brave Black Regiment*, 198.

63 "The first commission to a colored officer": *Weekly Anglo-African*, April 16, 1864.

63 "looked forward to the day": Ibid., April 23, 1864.

64 "color, he being partially of African blood": War Department Memorandum, in *The Black Military Experience*, vol. 2 of *Freedom: A Documentary History of Emancipation, 1861–1867*, ed. Ira Berlin (New York: Cambridge University Press, 1982), 345.

64 "Sergeant Stephen A. Swails is not yet mustered": Hallowell to Andrew, September 19, 1864, ibid., 493.

64 "Stephen Swails (Colored) is acting": Richard Allison to Headquarters, October 11, 1864, Stephen A. Swails, First Sergeant, Company F, 54th Massachusetts Infantry (Colored), Compiled Military Service Record, Record Group 94, National Archives, Washington, DC (hereafter Swails Compiled Military Service Record).

65 "commissioned as a 2nd Lieutenant": Swails Compiled Military Service Record, quoted in Hugh MacDougall, "The Search for Stephen Swails" (unpublished article, April 2004), 28.

65 "respectfully ask a Discharge": Swails to Department Headquarters, October 15, 1864, in Berlin, *Black Military Experience*, 342.

65 "1st Sergeant Stephen A. Swails is hereby relieved": Order, October 18, 1864, Swails Compiled Military Service Record.

65 "decided that [Swails] could not be mustered": Berlin, *Black Military Experience*, 343.

65 "of white Caucasian blood": Endorsement of Governor Andrew, December 2, 1864, ibid., 343–44.

66 "Sergeant Swails is so nearly white": Foster letter, January 15, 1865, ibid., 345.

66 "to discharge Sergeant S. A. Swails": Ibid.

66 "This decision, persistently solicited": Emilio, *Brave Black Regiment*, 268.

66 "much feeling in the Regiment": James A. Trotter quoted in Trudeau, *Like Men of War*, 374.

66 "The day of departure was delightful": Emilio, *Brave Black Regiment*, 184–85.

67 "Our daily duties of fatigue": Ibid., 197.

67 "there was little to remind us of the old pathway": Ibid., 200.

67 "became almost unbearable": Ibid., 204.

67 "choosing to endure the odor": Frederick Denison, *Shot and Shell: The Third Rhode Island Heavy Artillery Regiment in the War of the Rebellion* (Providence, RI: J. A. and R. A. Reid, 1879), 255.

68 "premeditated plan, originating somewhere": "Treatment of Prisoners of War by the Rebel Authorities," in James F. Rhodes, *History of the United States*, vol. 5, *1864–1865* (New York: Macmillan, 1920), 503–4.

68   "tall, lank mountaineers": Emilio, *Brave Black Regiment,* 222–23.

69   "such attentions and politeness": Ibid., 226.

CHAPTER SIX

Crowned with Laurels

78   "break the Charleston and Savannah Railroad": Sherman to Halleck, November 11, 1864, quoted in Emilio, *Brave Black Regiment,* 236.

78   "it is said that the guide": Ibid., 239.

78   "The generalship displayed was not equal": *Philadelphia Weekly Times,* May 17, 1884.

79   "with joyful demonstrations": Emilio, *Brave Black Regiment,* 278.

79   "We are all destitute of clothes": Sgt. John Collins quoted in Redkey, *Grand Army of Black Men,* 71.

79   "Cheer after cheer rang out": Emilio, *Brave Black Regiment,* 279.

79   "Being the first considerable body": Ibid., 280.

79   "There, across the river": Ibid.

79   "On the day we entered that rebellious city": Sergeant Collins quoted in Redkey, *Grand Army of Black Men,* 78–79.

80   "I hear on all sides": Gillmore to Hatch, March 1, 1865, *OR,* 47(2):641.

80   "the privations of the white soldiers": Quoted in Emilio, *Brave Black Regiment,* app., 412.

81   "2,500 men lightly equipped": Sherman to Gillmore, March 15, 1865, *OR,* 47(2):856–57. Sumterville is modern-day Sumter, South Carolina.

81   "The country we passed through": Edward L. Stevens diary, April 5, 1865, in *The Illustrated Recollections of Potter's Raid, April 5–21, 1865,* ed. Allan D. Thigpen (Sumter, SC: Gamecock City Printing, 1998), 45.

82   "Little boys and girls": Ibid., 47.

82   "We must have burned": Ibid., 263.

83   "I'll shoot the first man": Tom Elmore, *Potter's Raid through South Carolina: The Final Days of the Confederacy* (Charleston, SC: History, 2015), 49.

83   "destroyed all the railway buildings": Potter's Report, April 26, 1865, *OR,* 47(1):1026.

83   "The negroes had flocked to us": Edward C. Culp, *25th Ohio Veteran Volunteer Infantry in the War for the Union* (Topeka, KS: G. W. Crane, 1885), 126.

84   "Scarcely had we accomplished the passage": Charles E. Tucker quoted in Emilio, *Brave Black Regiment,* 297.

84   "The great, great emancipation of hundreds of thousands": Edward Stevens diary, April 14, 1865, in Thigpen, *Illustrated Recollections of Potter's Raid,* 423.

84   "The heroes of Wagner and Olustee": Joseph T. Wilson, *The Black Phalanx* (New York: Da Capo, 1994), 278.

85   "Do you think you can stop him?": Elmore, *Potter's Raid through South Carolina,* 69.

85   "The explosion was terrific": Culp, *25th Ohio Veteran Volunteer Infantry,* 132.

85   "The men were allowed frequent passes": Emilio, *Brave Black Regiment,* 312.

86   "she had no knowledge": Susan Aspinall Swails Affidavit, 1900, Stephen A. Swails, Pension Records, Entry 15, Record Group 15, Pension Records, National Archives, Washington, DC.

86   "First Lieutenant Swails is hereby detailed": Andrew Order, July 1, 1865, Swails Personal Papers.

86   "Everywhere along the route": Emilio, *Brave Black Regiment,* 319.

87   "The Fifty-fourth Massachusetts Regiment": *Boston Evening Transcript,* September 3, 1865.

CHAPTER SEVEN

This Is a White Man's Government

88   "fashioned our modes of life": Mitchell Snay, *Gospel of Disunion: Religion and Separatism in the Antebellum South* (Chapel Hill: University of North Carolina Press, 1997), 177.

88   "every Negro in South Carolina": James Furman, letter to the Citizens of the Greenville District, in *Greenville Southern Enterprise,* November 22, 1860.

88   "some of the most eminent": Rev. Alexander McCaine quoted in Snay, *Gospel of Disunion,* 57.

89   "the most blessed and beautiful form": *Central Presbyterian,* March 22, 1856.

89   "a relation essential to the existence": Ibid., January 28, 1860

89   "both Christianity and Slavery": *Christian Index,* February 13, 1861.

89   "without indignation and horror": Stephen F. Hale to Gov. Beriah Magoffin, December 27, 1860, in Charles B. Dew, *Apostles of Disunion: Southern Secession Commissioners and the Causes of the Civil War* (Charlottesville: University Press of Virginia, 2001), 122–25.

89   "the black race will be in a large majority": Henry L. Benning quoted in Dew, *Apostles of Disunion,* 66–67.

89   "the turning loose upon society": Hon. John Townsend, *The Doom of Slavery in the Union,* October 29, 1860 (pamphlet).

91   "black hair and luxurious English whiskers": Whitelaw Reid, *After the War: A Southern Tour* (New York: Moore, Wilstach, and Baldwin, 1866), 80.

91   "Many of the farms and plantations had suffered": Martin Abbott, *The Freedmen's Bureau in South Carolina, 1865–1872* (Chapel Hill: University of North Carolina Press, 1967), 11

92   "To my native infamy as a Yankee": John William DeForest, *A Union Officer in the Reconstruction* (New Haven, CT: Yale University Press, 1948), xviii.

92   "an army of malignant Southern haters": *Charleston Mercury,* December 17, 1867.

92   "the late rebels hate and slander us": Saxton to Howard, September 9, 1865, quoted in Abbott, *Freedmen's Bureau in South Carolina,* 116.

93   "The African has been": *Charleston Daily Courier,* October 1, 1866, quoted in

Thomas Holt, *Black over White: Negro Political Leadership in South Carolina during Reconstruction* (Urbana: University of Illinois Press, 1979), 25.

94 "Many coats [worn by the convention's attendees] showed Confederate buttons": Sidney Andrews, *The South since the War: Fourteen Weeks of Travel and Observation in Georgia and the Carolinas* (Boston: Ticknor and Fields, 1866), 40.

94 "are not entitled to social or political equality": Details of the Black Codes are from John S. Reynolds, *Reconstruction in South Carolina, 1865–1877* (Columbia, SC: State, 1905), 27–31.

95 "bore varied responsibilities": DeForest, *Union Officer in the Reconstruction*, xvi.

96 "the whole thing originated from fear": *New York Times*, December 30, 1866.

96 "the feelings of the [white] people about Kingstree": Ibid.

97 "that you have driven him off the plantation": Swails to Dr. Cunningham, June 27, 1867, Records of the Field Offices for the State South Carolina, Bureau of Refugees, Freedmen, and Abandoned Lands, 1865–1872, Kingstree, South Carolina, Roll 85, Letters Sent, January 1867–December 1868, National Archives, Washington, DC.

97 "you have discharged him": Swails letter, July 31, 1867, ibid.

97 "Clem Watson, an old freedman": Swails letter, July 3, 1867, ibid.

98 "send the heads of families": Swails letter, August 16, 1867.

98 "had a woman on his plantation": Swails letter, August 28, 1867, ibid.

98 "the Planters to furnish the said freedmen with permissions": Swails letter, September 6, 1867, ibid.

98 "Sam Wilson (Freedman) makes a complaint": Swails letter, September 5, 1867, ibid.

98 "give the parties the two-thirds as was agreed": Swails letter, September 26, 1867, ibid.

98 "you are wronging these people": Swails letter, October 1, 1867, ibid.

98 "visit the plantation of Mr. Bennett Gordon": Swails letter, October 2, 1867, ibid.

99 "a great many troublesome cases": Swails letter, September 11, 1867, ibid.

99 "were frivolous . . . and thrown out": Swails letter, September 28, 1867, ibid.

CHAPTER EIGHT
The Political Boss of Williamsburg County

100 "Give the negro political equality": Richard Zuczek, *State of Rebellion: Reconstruction in South Carolina* (Columbia: University of South Carolina Press, 1996), 37.

101 "as citizens of the United States": Reynolds, *Reconstruction in South Carolina*, 76.

101 "A Radical ticket was nominated": *Kingstree (SC) Star*, n.d., quoted in the *Charleston Daily News*, November 15, 1867.

102 "They are the best debaters": *New York Times*, January 21, 1868.

102 "against the rules of his room to permit them to play": *Charleston Mercury*, March 18, 1868.

103 "all men are born free and equal": SC Const. of 1868, art. I.

104 "negro rule and supremacy": Reynolds, *Reconstruction in South Carolina*, 91.

104   "negro constitution, of a negro government": Henry D. Green quoted in Walter
      Edgar, *South Carolina: A History* (Columbia: University of South Carolina Press
      1998), 386.

104   "the effect is that the new constitution establishes": Reynolds, *Reconstruction
      in South Carolina,* 93–94.

105   "the assured success of the reconstruction policy": "Republican Party Platform
      of 1868," May 20, 1868, *American Presidency Project,* https://www.presidency.
      ucsb.edu/documents/republican-party-platform-1868.

105   "a semi-barbarous race of blacks": Eric Foner, *A Short History of Reconstruction*
      (New York: Harper Collins, 2014), 145.

105   "was discovered by the white man": Armistead Burt quoted in Joel Williamson,
      After Slavery: The Negro in South Carolina during Reconstruction, 1861–1877
      (Chapel Hill: University of North Carolina Press, 1965), 73.

105   "peaceful and unoffending citizens": Proclamation of Gov. Robert K. Scott, Octo-
      ber 20, 1868, in *Testimony Taken by the Joint Select Committee to Inquire into
      the Condition of Affairs in the Late Insurrectionary States,* vol. 11, *South Carolina*
      (Washington, DC: Government Printing Office, 1872), 1254–55.

106   "the killing of Mr. Dill": George F. Price, 1st lieutenant, 5th US Cavalry, to Louis V.
      Caziarc, Assistant Adjutant General, June 22, 1868, in *Annual Report of the Secre-
      tary of War,* vol. 1 (Washington, DC: Government Printing Office, 1868), 467–73,
      quoted in Stephen Berry, *Birth of a Conscience,* eHistory, May 31, 2019, https://
      csidixie.org/chronicles/birth-conscience.

106   "bitter enemy of the white race": *Charleston Courier* quoted in Berry, "Birth of a
      Conscience."

106   "incendiary and threatening speeches": *Orangeburg (SC) News,* October 24, 1868.

106   "the destruction of the Republican party": Francis B. Simpkins, "The Ku Klux
      Klan in South Carolina, 1868–1871," *Journal of Negro History* 12, no. 4 (October
      1927): 609.

106   "a body which represents": *Edgefield (SC) Advertiser,* November 4, 1864.

108   "an educated Negro": William Willis Bodie, *Narrative of History of Williams-
      burg: Something about the People of Williamsburg County, South Carolina, from
      the First Settlement by Europeans about 1705 until 1923* (Columbia, SC: State,
      1923), 446–47.

108   "the political 'boss' of Williamsburg County": Eric Foner, *Freedom's Lawmakers:
      A Directory of Black Officeholders during Reconstruction,* rev. ed. (Baton Rouge:
      Louisiana State University Press, 1996), 207.

109   "the hospitalities of our excellent State Senator": W. D. Harris, in *The Christian
      Recorder,* quoted in MacDougall, "Search for Stephen Swails," 11.

111   "creating a general reign of terror": Scott to Grant, n.d., quoted in Zuczek, *State
      of Rebellion,* 90.

111   "stupid leading darkies": W. R. Robertson to A. B. Springs, August 23, 1870, quoted
      in Zuczek, *State of Rebellion,* 80.

111   "conspire or go in disguise": An Act to Enforce the Provisions of the Fourteenth

Amendment to the Constitution of the United States, and for other Purposes, 42nd Cong., sess. 1, CH. 22 (1871).

112   "force and terror": Ulysses S. Grant quoted in Herbert Shapiro, "The Ku Klux Klan during Reconstruction: The South Carolina Episode," *Journal of Negro History* 49, no. 1 (January 1964): 43.

112   "No one can imagine the sufferings": *New York Tribune,* May 31, June 8, November 10, 1871, quoted in Shapiro, "Ku Klux Klan during Reconstruction," 47.

112   "impossible for me to explain": Ibid.

112   "was shot and instantly killed": Swails to Governor Scott, July 26, 1871, Letters Received, Governor Robert K. Scott (1868–1872), South Carolina Department of Archives and History, Columbia.

113   "very strong character": Monroe N. Work et al., "Some Negro Members of Reconstruction Conventions and Legislatures and of Congress," *Journal of Negro History* 5, no. 1 (January 1920): 98.

113   "it is also currently reported": Swails to Governor Scott, June 28, 1868, Letters Received, Governor Robert K. Scott.

114   "any distinction in the admission of students": Quoted in Benjamin Ginsberg, *Moses of South Carolina: A Jewish Scalawag during Radical Reconstruction* (Baltimore: Johns Hopkins University Press, 2010), 158.

114   "go up the spout": Williamson, *After Slavery,* 232.

114   "commendable dignity": Daniel W. Hollis, *University of South Carolina,* vol. 2 (Columbia: University of South Carolina Press, 1956), 67.

114   "defilement": Reynolds, *Reconstruction in South Carolina,* 236.

115   "such pupils when admitted": JoAnn Michell Brasington, *The South Carolina School for the Deaf and the Blind, 1849–2 000* (s.n., 2000), 4.

115   "To a substantial extent": Ginsberg, *Moses of South Carolina,* 118.

CHAPTER NINE

A Campaign of Intimidation and Terror

116   "the great bribe taker": *Keowee (SC) Courier,* October 31, 1878.

117   "dedicate themselves to the redemption": Hampton quoted in the *Edgefield (SC) Advertiser,* November 7, 1872.

117   "the hell-born policy": *Fairfield (SC) Herald,* November 20, 1972.

117   "the worse corruption and abuse": Zuczek, *State of Rebellion,* 135.

117   "Millions have been stolen": Paul Hamilton Hayne quoted in Zuczek, *State of Rebellion,* 136.

118   "Swails, who is a brigadier of militia": Quoted in Egerton, *Thunder at the Gates,* 327.

118   "hailed with Thanksgiving in South Carolina": Belton O'Neall Townsend, "The Political Condition of South Carolina," *Atlantic Monthly* 39 (February 1877): 182.

119   "a horrible disaster": Chamberlain to President Grant, January 4, 1876, quoted in Reynolds, *Reconstruction in South Carolina,* 323.

119   "Moses shall never take his seat": *Charleston News and Courier,* January 5, 1876.

119   "A minority of white men": A. M. Speights quoted in *Spartanburg (SC) Herald,* April 5, 1876.

120   "Gentlemen of the convention": Quotations from the meeting are from *New York Times,* April 12, 1876; and *Beaufort (SC) Tribune,* April 19, 1876.

121   "He was a big, powerful, athletic man": Walter Brian Cisco, *Wade Hampton: Confederate Warrior, Conservative Statesman* (Washington, DC: Brassey's, 2004), 239.

121   "Oh, my watch has stopped": Ibid., 238.

122   "Treat them as to show them": Martin Gary quoted in Zuczek, *State of Rebellion,* 167.

122   "was not that of a candidate": Ibid., 173.

122   "radiant young woman": Alfred B. Williams, *Hampton and His Red Shirts: South Carolina's Deliverance in 1876* (Charleston, SC: Walker, Evans, and Cogswell, 1935), 244.

123   "A thousand men on horseback": Reynolds, *Reconstruction in South Carolina,* 357–58.

123   "truly deplorable": Trial Justice Black to Governor Chamberlain, October 2, 1876, Letters Received, Governor Daniel H. Chamberlain (1874–1877), South Carolina Department of Archives and History, Columbia.

123   "vote every white man": LaWanda Cox and John H. Cox, eds., *Reconstruction, the Negro, and the New South* (Columbia: University of South Carolina Press, 1973), 303–9.

124   "at one time it seemed that bloodshed": Zuczek, *State of Rebellion,* 195.

124   "The people have elected me Governor": Hampton quoted in Reynolds, *Reconstruction in South Carolina,* 425.

125   "unless Governor Chamberlain can compel": President Grant quoted in *New York Tribune,* February 18, 1877.

125   "By the order of the President": *Newberry (SC) Herald,* July 18, 1877; MacDougall, "Search for Stephen Swails," 43.

126   "The troops have been withdrawn": Cisco, *Wade Hampton,* 266.

126   "The slave went free": W. E. B. Du Bois, *Black Reconstruction in America: An Essay toward a History of the Part Which Black Folk Played in the Attempt to Reconstruct Democracy in America, 1860–1880* (New York: Harcourt, Brace, 1935), 30.

126   "The primary purpose of the legislative committee": Edgar, *South Carolina,* 409–10.

127   "Troops of red-shirts have ridden up": *New York Times,* October 16, 1878.

127   "Swails is a mulatto carpet-bagger": *Newberry (SC) Weekly Herald,* December 5, 1877.

127   "apathy, fear, and defeatism": Holt, *Black over White,* 213.

127   "organized a campaign of intimidation": *New York Times,* October 18, 1878.

128   "the most prominent Republican": Ibid.

128   "we must stand together": Swails to Hampton, October 7, 1878, Swails Personal

Papers. Swails's entire account of the White Oak incident is also reproduced in *New York Times,* October 16, 1878.

129   "You have done a great deal of harm": Montgomery to President, October 17, 1878, Swails Personal Papers.

129   "Go on": Swails to Hampton, October 7, 1878, ibid.

CHAPTER TEN

What a Mockery of Justice Is This?

132   "a resolute man, nearly white": *Janesville (WI) Daily Gazette,* October 15, 1878.

132   "the Democrats, uniformed in Red Shirts": *New York Times,* October 15, 1878.

132   "Mr. Swails called the attention of the President": *Janesville (WI) Daily Gazette,* October 15, 1878.

132   "This man Swails was for a long time president pro tem": *Baltimore Sun,* October 16, 1878.

133   "slanders"; "gang of copper-colored": *Washington Post,* October 25, 1878.

134   "simple statement is enough": *Anderson (SC) Intelligencer,* October 31, 1878.

134   "Although the Republicans have large majorities": *Indianapolis News,* October 23, 1878.

134   "the exact time in which he (Swails) will leave": *Boston Journal* article reproduced in the *Fitchburg (SC) Sentinel,* November 14, 1879.

134   "forthwith upon peril to his life": Swails to Hampton, October 7, 1878, Swails Personal Papers.

135   "While I depreciate all acts of violence": Hampton to Swails, October 24, 1878, ibid. This letter is also in *New York Times,* October 31, 1878.

135   "direct and notorious falsehood": *Reading (PA) Times,* November 1, 1878.

136   "To tell Republican sufferers that the courts are open": *New York Times,* October 31, 1878.

136   "As you have seen fit to attack me": Hirsch to Swails, May 20, 1877, Swails Personal Papers.

136   "As I expected and as I told Governor Hampton": Swails to Sheriff Jacobs, November 15, 1878, ibid.

137   "interfering with Swails in his advocacy": *Philadelphia Times,* October 28, 1878.

137   "The Democrats refused the United States Supervisor admission": *New York Times,* January 23, 1879.

137   "some of the niggers voted the Democratic ticket": White quoted in *Stevens Point (WI) Daily Journal,* November 30, 1878; and in MacDougall, "Search for Stephen Swails," 46.

138   "colored children, thirty or forty of them": White quoted in *The Nation,* November 21, 1878, 309.

138   "I went to your house and packed them": Jacobs to Swails, November 12, 1877, Swails Personal Papers.

138   "The white people": *Kingstree (SC) Star,* July 1879, quoted in *National Republican* (Washington, DC), July 12, 1879.

139   "In the County of Williamsburg": *New York Times,* October 21, 1878.

139   "His property is all in the hands of Sheriff Jacobs": *Kingstree (SC) Star,* n.d., quoted in *National Republican* (Washington, DC), July 12, 1879.

139   "Hearing that he was about to return": *Bangor (ME) Daily Whig and Courier,* July 31, 1879, quoted in *New York Times,* August 10, 1879.

140   "most bitter and diabolical": *Kingstree (SC) Star,* n.d., quoted in *Orangeburg (SC) Democrat,* August 11, 1880.

140   "has returned to Williamsburg": *Newberry (SC) Herald,* August 11, 1880.

140   "It took us entirely by surprise": *Kingstree (SC) Star,* n.d., quoted in *Orangeburg (SC) Democrat,* August 11, 1880.

140   "have decided once again": *Anderson (SC) Intelligencer,* August 12, 1880.

140   "The notorious S. A. Swails": *Yorkville (SC) Enquirer,* September 15, 1881.

141   "announcing his intention to canvas": *Sumter (SC) Watchman and Southron,* February 26, 1884.

142   "The reason given for his dismissal": *National Tribune* (Washington, DC), March 4, 1886.

142   "a serious riot between the whites and blacks": *Fairfield (SC) News and Herald,* September 28, 1887.

142   "the freest and fairest in the world": Ibid., October 10, 1888.

143   "the most enthusiastic that has been seen": *Yorkville (SC) Enquirer,* October 3, 1888.

CHAPTER ELEVEN

A Proper Denouement to an Extraordinary Man

145   "Give this colored man, this former slave": Robert M. LaFollette quoted in Edward A. Miller Jr., *Gullah Statesman: Robert Smalls, from Slavery to Congress, 1839–1915* (Columbia: University of South Carolina Press, 1995), 169.

145   "Reports of your success in South Carolina": George Pope to Swails, December 5, 1880, Swails Personal Papers.

146   "In complying with this request": Joseph T. Wilson to Swails, August 1, 1883, ibid.

146   "I am requested by Colonel N. P. Hallowell": William Dufnee to Swails, May 12, 1897, ibid.

146   "for surgery and rest cure": Sanitarium receipt, March 9, 1899, ibid.

147   "in very bad shape": Henry A. Cauth to F. Grant Swails, March 10, 1899, ibid.

147   "so glad to hear you were improving": George A. Cooper to Swails, April 1, 1899, ibid.

147   "news of your recovery": George W. Jackson to Swails, April 1, 1899, ibid.

147   "acute dysentery": Dr. D. C. Scott quoted in Egerton, *Thunder at the Gates,* 329.

147 "S. A. Swails, who figured so prominently": *Williamsburg (SC) County Record,* May 2, 1900.

148 "S.A. Swails, a colored soldier": Samuel D. McGill, *Narrative of Reminiscences in Williamsburg County* (Columbia, SC: Bryan Printing, 1897), 223.

149 "There came out of Potter's Raiders": Bodie, *History of Williamsburg County,* 446–47.

149 "led a successful movement for the expulsion": Henry E. Davis quoted in Robert Witherspoon et al., *Williamsburg Presbyterian Church, 1736–1881* (Kingstree, SC: Williamsburg Presbyterian Church, 1981), 78.

150 "proper denouement to an extraordinary man": *Kingstree (SC) News,* February 10, 2014.

150 "to the wellbeing of the citizens of South Carolina": South Carolina Legislature, S.1419, A Senate Resolution Authorizing the Commissioning of a Portrait of the Honorable Stephen Atkins Swails to be Placed in the Senate Chamber, June 4, 2008.

150 "No veteran of the three black regiments": Egerton, *Thunder at the Gates,* 323–24.

Epilogue

152 "As a result of their service": Colin Powell, "A Black Soldier Reflects," October 5, 1997, 54th Massachusetts Volunteer Infantry Regiment Company B, http://www.54thmass.org/a-black-soldier-reflects/.

153 "triumph of democracy and white supremacy": Benjamin Tillman, quoted in Edgar, *South Carolina,* 438.

153 "have never recognized the right": Ibid., 445.

NOTE ON SOURCES

CHAPTER ONE
An Angel of God Come Down to Lead the Host of Freedom

The frequently contentious relations between Blacks and whites in the North before the Civil War has received scant attention. I found Thomas P. Slaughter, *Bloody Dawn: the Christiana Riot and Racial Violence in the Antebellum North* (New York: Oxford University Press, 1991), especially enlightening. It contains an excellent analysis of the 1834 riots in Columbia, Pennsylvania. The Columbia riots, their causes, and their aftermath are also detailed in William Frederic Worner, "The Columbia Race Riots of 1834 and 1835," in *Historical Papers and Addresses of the Lancaster County Historical Society*, vol. 26 (Lancaster, 1922), 175–87; and Leroy T. Hopkins, "Black Eldorado on the Susquehanna: The Emergence of Black Columbia, 1726–1861," *Journal of the Lancaster County Historical Society* 89, no. 4 (1985): 110–32.

The most comprehensive modern treatment of the Underground Railroad is Fergus M. Bordewich, *Bound for Canaan: The Epic Story of the Underground Railroad, America's First Civil Rights Movement* (New York: Amistad, 2005). Also instructive are Robert C. Smedley, *The History of the Underground Railroad in Chester and the Neighboring Counties of Pennsylvania* (Lancaster, PA: The Journal, 1883); William J. Switala, *Underground Railroad in Pennsylvania* (Mechanicsburg, PA: Stackpole Books, 2001); and William Still, *The Underground Railroad* (Chicago: Johnson, 1970).

Information about Stephen Swails's early years is scant. My account relies heavily on the meticulous research undertaken by Hugh MacDougall of Cooperstown, New York, a retired attorney and diplomat who spent several years collecting material pertinent to Swails. His unpublished article "The Search for Stephen Swails" (completed in April 2004) presents what little is known about Swails's sojourn in Columbia, Manheim, Elmira, and Cooperstown, relying predominantly on US Census documents. Information about Swails's parents comes from the US Census for Columbia Township, Lancaster County, Pennsylvania, during their residency there. The debate in 1868 over Swails's conduct in Cooperstown is from "Kinder and Gentler: An Exchange between Two Cooperstown, N.Y., Weeklies, 1868," *New York History* 71, no. 3 (July 1992): 375–80.

The seminal account of the 54th Massachusetts is Lewis F. Emilio, *A Brave Black Regiment: History of the Fifty-Fourth Regiment of Massachusetts Volunteer Infantry, 1863–1865* (Boston: Boston Book, 1894). Not only was Emilio a major figure in the 54th, but after the war, he collected reminiscences from scores of his fellow officers and soldiers. For modern analyses, see Dudley Taylor Cornish, *The Sable Arm: Black Troops in the Union Army, 1861–1865* (Lawrence: University Press of Kansas, 1987); Noah A. Trudeau, *Like Men of War: Black Troops in the Civil War, 1862–1865* (Boston: Little, Brown,1998); Martin H. Blatt et al., eds., *Hope and Glory: Essays on the Legacy of the 54th Massachusetts Regiment* (Amherst: University of Massachusetts Press, 2009); and Douglas R. Egerton, *Thunder at the Gates: The Black Civil War Regiments That Redeemed America* (New York: Basic Books, 2016). Contemporary letters and recountings of life in the 54th Regiment are in Donald Yacovone, ed., *A Voice of Thunder: A Black Soldier's Civil War* (Urbana: University of Illinois Press, 1998), particularly George E. Stephens's accounts; Virginia M. Adams, *On the Altar of Freedom: A Black Soldier's Civil War Letters from the Front* (Amherst: University of Massachusetts Press, 1991), particularly James Henry Gooding's accounts; and Edwin S. Redkey, ed., *A Grand Army of Black Men: Letters from African-American Soldiers in the Union Army, 1861–1865* (New York: Cambridge University Press, 1992). For insight into how the African American community viewed volunteering for military service and the white community's reactions to Black military service, I recommend Brian Taylor, *Fighting for Citizenship: Black Northerners and the Debate over Military Service in the Civil War* (Chapel Hill: University of North Carolina Press, 2020), and Glenn David Brasher, "Debating Black Manhood: The Northern Press Reports on the 54th Massachusetts at Fort Wagner," in *American Discord: The Republic and Its People in the Civil War Era*, ed. Megan L. Bever, Lesley J. Gordon, and Laura Mammina (Baton Rouge: Louisiana State University Press, 2020), 22–44. Frederick Douglass's role in helping recruit volunteers for the 54th is recounted in David W. Blight, *Frederick Douglass: Prophet of Freedom* (New York: Simon and Schuster, 2018).

The definitive biography of Massachusetts governor John Andrew is Henry Greenleaf Pearson, *The Life of John A. Andrew*, 2 vols. (Boston: Houghton, Mifflin,1904). Several works touch on aspects of Robert Gould Shaw's life and his passion for the 54th Massachusetts. Most helpful are Russell Duncan, ed., *Blue-Eyed Child of Fortune: The Civil War Letters of Colonel Robert Gould Shaw* (Athens: University of Georgia Press, 1992), and Peter Burchard, *One Gallant*

Rush: Robert Gould Shaw and His Brave Black Regiment (New York: St. Martin's, 1965). Primary-source material abounds in the Massachusetts Historical Society in Boston, which contains Governor Andrew's personal papers and extensive documentation relating to the 54th Massachusetts. An invaluable primary source is the personal journal of John W. M. Appleton in the West Virginia and Regional History Center in Morristown. Information about Swails's initial involvement in the regiment and his physical appearance are collected in his personal papers. As the University of South Carolina has not catalogued the documents or otherwise listed them among its holdings, I have relied on copies in William "Billy" Jenkinson's personal collection in Kingstree, South Carolina. Also helpful was Stephen A. Swails, First Sergeant, Company F, 54th Massachusetts Infantry (Colored), Compiled Military Service Record, Record Group 94, National Archives, Washington, DC; and Stephen A. Swails, Pension Records, Entry 15, Record Group 15, Pension Records, National Archives.

CHAPTER TWO

One Plane of Ashes and Blackened Chimneys

Civil War operations along coastal South Carolina and Florida have received scant treatment. Details of those operations during the pertinent period are contained in the contemporaneous reports and communications of participants in US War Department, *The War of the Rebellion: A Compilation of Official Records of the Union and Confederate Armies,* 130 vols. (Washington, DC: Government Printing Office, 1880–1901), ser. 1, esp. vol. 14. Newspaper accounts are also invaluable, particularly those from the *Charleston Mercury,* the *New York Times,* and the *Boston Commonwealth.* The soundest modern analysis is Stephen R. Wise, *Gate of Hell: Campaign for Charleston Harbor, 1863* (Columbia: University of South Carolina Press, 1994). For details about Generals Hunter and Montgomery, see Edward A. Miller, *Lincoln's Abolitionist General: The Biography of David Hunter* (Columbia: University of South Carolina Press, 1997), and Christopher Looby, ed., *The Complete Civil War Journal and Selected Letters of Thomas Wentworth Higginson* (Chicago: University of Chicago Press, 2000). Hunter's letter to Jefferson Davis appears in Robert L. Hayman, *The Smart Culture: Society, Intelligence, and Laws* (New York: New York University Press, 1997), 60.

For an excellent description of wartime Port Royal, see Stephen R. Wise and Lawrence S. Rowland, *Rebellion, Reconstruction, and Redemption, 1861–1893: The History of Beaufort County, South Carolina* (Columbia: University of South Carolina Press, 2015), vol. 2. Descriptions of Montgomery's Combahee expedition and his destruction of Darian appear in Spencer B. King Jr., *Darien: The Death and Rebirth of a Southern Town* (Macon, GA: Mercer University Press, 1981), and Sarah H. Bradford, *Harriet: The Moses of Her People* (New York: Geo. R. Lockwood and Son, 1886).

CHAPTER THREE
Looking Out from among the Ghastly Corpses

Details of the 54th Massachusetts's engagements leading up to and including the assault on Fort Wagner are from the works cited for chapter 2, especially Wise, *Gate of Hell*. Additional sources include E. Milby Burton, *The Siege of Charleston, 1861–1865* (Columbia: University of South Carolina Press, 1970); Timothy Eugene Bradshaw Jr., *Battery Wagner: The Siege, the Men Who Fought, and the Casualties* (Columbia, SC: Palmetto Historical Works, 1993); John Appleton, "That Night at Fort Wagner, by One who Was There," *Putnam's Magazine* 4, no. 19 (July 1869): 9–16; Elbridge J. Copp, *Reminiscences of the War of the Rebellion, 1861–1865* (Nashua, NH: Telegraph, 1911); Alfred P. Rockwell, "The Operations against Charleston," in *Papers of the Military Historical Society of Massachusetts*, vol. 9 (Boston, 1912), 161–93; and Garth W. James, "The Assault on Fort Wagner," in Military Order of the Loyal Legion of the United States, *War Papers Read before the Commandery of the State of Wisconsin*, vol. 1 (Milwaukee: Burdick, Armitage, and Allen, 1891), 9–30. A brief but moving account of the Fort Wagner offensive and its aftermath is in Robert N. Rosen, *Confederate Charleston: An Illustrated History of the City and The People Firing the Civil War* (Columbia: University of South Carolina Press, 1994). Detailed reports and communications by the participants are in *War of the Rebellion*, vol. 28, pts. 1–2.

CHAPTER FOUR
Why Can't We Have a Soldier's Pay?

Details of the siege and ultimate capture of Forts Wagner and Gregg are described in the works cited above, especially Wise, *Gate of Hell;* Emilio, *Brave Black Regiment;* Yacovone, *Voice of Thunder;* Adams, *On the Alter of Freedom;* and Burton, *Siege of Charleston.* Detailed reports in *War of the Rebellion*, vol. 28, document the siege day by day. Interesting accounts of the siege by soldiers in the 55th Massachusetts, which joined the 54th on August 3, are in W. Robert Beckman and Sharon S. MacDonald, *Carrying the Colors: The Life and Legacy of Medal of Honor Recipient Andrew Jackson Smith* (Yardley, PA: Westholme, 2020); Noah Andre Trudeau, *Voices of the 55th: Letters from the 55th Massachusetts Volunteers, 1861-1865* (Dayton, OH: Morningside House, 1996); and Charles B. Bowditch, "War Letters of Charles B. Bowditch," *Massachusetts Historical Society Proceedings* 57 (1924): 414-95.

Efforts by members of the 54th Massachusetts to receive the pay they had been promised are related in detail in Emilio, *Brave Black Regiment;* Yacovone, *Voice of Thunder;* Redkey, *Grand Army of Black Men;* Virginia M. Adams, ed., *On the Altar of Freedom: A Black Soldier's Civil War Letters from the Front* (Amherst: University of Massachusetts Press, 1991); and MacDougall, "Search for Stephen Swails" (unpublished). See also Ira Berlin et al., "Writing Freedom's History," *Prologue* 14, no. 3 (Fall 1982), 211-27. Information concerning the Confederates' treatment of Black prisoners and Lincoln's response is in Emilio, *Brave Black Regiment;* Wise, *Gate of Hell;* Rosen, *Confederate Charleston;* and *Charleston Mercury,* August 12-15, 1863.

CHAPTER FIVE

I Can Now Recommend His Being Allowed to
Serve as a Commissioned Officer

The two best accounts of the Florida expedition and the Battle of Olustee are Robert P. Broadwater, *The Battle of Olustee, 1864: The Final Union Attempt to Seize Florida* (Jefferson, NC: McFarland, 1958), and William H. Nulty, *Confederate Florida: The Road to Olustee* (Tuscaloosa: University of Alabama Press, 1990). Excellent descriptions of the operation are also in James H. Clark, *The Iron Hearted Regiment: Being an Account of the Battles, Marches and Gallant Deeds Performed by the 115th Regiment N.Y. Volunteers* (New York: Thomson Gale, 1865); Tyler Dennett, ed., *Lincoln and the Civil War in the Diaries and Letters of John Hay* (New York: Dodd, Mead, 1939); and Massachusetts Adjutant General's Office, *Massachusetts Soldiers, Sailors, and Marines in the Civil War,* 8 vols. (Boston: Norwood, 1932), vol. 4. Reports by participants are in *War of the Rebellion,* vol. 35.

Details of Swails's fight to receive his officer's commission are recounted in MacDougall, "Search for Stephen Swails" (unpublished); Emilio, *Brave Black Regiment;* Ian Delahanty, "'So Nearly White': The Fight to Commission a Black Officer," We're History, May 21, 2015, werehistory.org/swails/; Ira Berlin, ed., *The Black Military Experience,* vol. 2 of *Freedom: A Documentary History of Emancipation, 1861-1867* (New York: Cambridge University Press, 1982); Joseph T. Glatthaar, *Forged in Battle: The Civil War Alliance of Black Soldiers and White*

Officers (New York: Free Press, 1990); and Swails, Compiled Military Service Record, National Archives. For a recounting of the treatment of prisoners of war and the internment of Union prisoners on Morris Island, see Karen Stokes, *The Immortal 600: Surviving Civil War Charleston and Savannah* (Charleston, SC: History, 2013).

CHAPTER SIX
Crowned with Laurels

Details of Potter's Raid are from Tom Elmore, *Potter's Raid through South Carolina: The Final Days of the Confederacy* (Charleston, SC: History, 2015); Allan D. Thigpen, ed., *The Illustrated Recollections of Potter's Raid, April 5–21, 1865* (Sumter, SC: Gamecock City, 1998); John Hammond Moore, ed., "The Last Officer—April 1865," *South Carolina Historical Magazine* 67, no. 1 (January 1966): 1–14; and Joseph T. Wilson, *The Black Phalanx: African American Soldiers in the War of Independence, the War of 1812, and the Civil War* (New York: Da Capo, 1994). Reports and communications of the participants are in *War of the Rebellion,* vol. 47, pt. 1. For the part the 54th Massachusetts played in the raid, see Emilio, *Brave Black Regiment,* and Leonne M. Hudson, "The Role of the 54th Massachusetts Regiment in Potter's Raid," *Historical Journal of Massachusetts* vol. 29, no. 2 (Summer 2002): 181–97. See also Swails Pension Records and Swails Compiled Service Record. Swails's sailing manifest is in *Charleston Daily Courier,* September 20, 1865.

CHAPTER SEVEN
This Is a White Man's Government

Descriptions of white Southerners' attitudes toward slavery and African Americans before and during the Civil War are from Mitchell Snay, *Gospel of Disunion: Religion and Separatism in the Antebellum South* (Chapel Hill: University of North Carolina Press, 1997), and Charles B. Dew, *Apostles of Disunion: Southern Secession Commissioners and the Causes of the Civil War* (Charlottesville: University Press of Virginia, 2001). My description of the Freedmen's Bureau is based largely on Martin Abbott, *The Freedmen's Bureau in South Carolina, 1865–1872* (Chapel Hill: University of North Carolina Press, 1967); George Bentley, *History of the Freedmen's Bureau* (Philadelphia: University of Pennsylvania Press, 1955); John William DeForest, *A Union Officer in the Reconstruction* (New

Haven, CT: Yale University Press, 1948); and John Porter Hollis, *The Early Period of Reconstruction in South Carolina* (Baltimore: Johns Hopkins Press, 1905).

Information about Reconstruction generally is drawn predominantly from Eric Foner, *A Short History of Reconstruction, 1863–1867* (New York: Harper Perennial, 2014); Foner, *Freedom's Lawmakers: A Directory of Black Officeholders during Reconstruction,* rev. ed. (Baton Rouge: Louisiana State University Press, 1996); Howard N. Rabinowitz, ed., *Southern Black Leaders of the Reconstruction Era* (Urbana: University of Illinois Press, 1982); Bruce Baker, ed., *After Slavery: Race, Labor, and Citizenship in the Reconstruction South* (Gainesville: University Press of Florida, 2013); John Richard Dennett, *The South as It Is: 1865–1866* (Tuscaloosa: University of Alabama Press, 2010); and Stephen Berry, "Birth of a Conscience," eHistory, May 31, 2019, https://csidixie.org/chronicles/birth-conscience.

For information concerning Reconstruction in South Carolina, I relied heavily on Walter Edgar, *South Carolina: A History* (Columbia: University of South Carolina Press, 1998); Willie Lee Rose, *Rehearsal for Reconstruction: The Port Royal Experiment* (New York: Vintage Books, 1964); Thomas Holt, *Black over White: Negro Political Leadership in South Carolina during Reconstruction* (Urbana: University of Illinois Press, 1979); John S. Reynolds, *Reconstruction in South Carolina, 1865–1877* (Columbia, SC: State, 1905); Richard Zuczek, *State of Rebellion: Reconstruction in South Carolina* (Columbia: University of South Carolina, 1996); Sidney Andrews, *The South since the War: As Shown by Fourteen Weeks of Travel and Observation in Georgia and the Carolinas* (Boston: Ticknor and Fields, 1866); and Berry, "Birth of a Conscience."

Swails's tenure with the Freemen's Bureau in Kingstree is well documented in his correspondence and memoranda contained in Records of the Field Offices for the State South Carolina, Bureau of Refugees, Freedmen, and Abandoned Lands, 1865–1872, Kingstree, South Carolina, Roll 85, Letters Sent, January 1867–December 1868, Freedmen's Bureau Collection, National Archives, Washington, DC. Details of incidents in Kingstree in the two years before Swails arrived are drawn largely from research in local newspapers performed by Linda Brown, a retired Kingstree newspaper editor and paralegal.

CHAPTER EIGHT
The Political Boss of Williamsburg County

Political developments in South Carolina during the period covered in this chapter are examined at length in Edgar, *South Carolina;* Holt, *Black over White;*

and Zuczek, *State of Rebellion*. Additional information and perspectives are in Benjamin Ginsberg, *Moses of South Carolina: A Jewish Scalawag during Radical Reconstruction* (Baltimore: Johns Hopkins University Press, 2010); Monroe N. Work et al., "Some Negro Members of Reconstruction Conventions and Legislatures and of Congress," *Journal of Negro History* 5, no. 1 (January 1920): 63–119; Joel Williamson, *After Slavery: The Negro in South Carolina during Reconstruction* (Chapel Hill: University of South Carolina Press, 1965); Carol Blesser, *The Promised Land: The History of the South Carolina Land Commission, 1869–1890* (Columbia: University of South Carolina Press, 1969), 64, 97; Bernard E. Powers Jr., "South Carolina Land Commission," South Carolina Encyclopedia, August 1, 2016, http://www.scencyclopedia.org/sce/entries/south-carolina-land-commission/; and Belton O'Neall Townsend, "The Political Condition of South Carolina," *Atlantic Monthly* 39 (February 1, 1877): 182.

The saga of the Ku Klux Klan in South Carolina is thoroughly documented in Francis B. Simpkins, "The Ku Klux Klan in South Carolina, 1868–1871," *Journal of Negro History* 12, no. 4 (October 1927): 606–47; and Herbert Shapiro, "The Ku Klux Klan during Reconstruction: the South Carolina Episode," *Journal of Negro History* 49, no. 1 (January 1964): 34–55.

References to Swails are from Swails Personal Papers and from William Willis Bodie, *History of Williamsburg: Something about the People of Williamsburg County, South Carolina, from the First Settlement by Europeans about 1705 until 1923* (Columbia, SC: State, 1923); Work et al., "Some Negro Members of Reconstruction Conventions and Legislatures and of Congress"; N. Louis Bailey et al., *Biographical Directory of the South Carolina Senate, 1776–1985*, vol. 3 (Columbia: University of South Carolina Press, 1986), 1570–72; William E. Jenkinson III, *Stephen A. Swails: Soldier, Politician, and Lawyer* (Williamsburgh, SC: Historical Society, 1998); and Office of the Clerk for Williamsburg County, Deed Book L, p. 158. For Swails's letters to Governors Scott, Moses, Chamberlain, and Hampton, see the papers of those governors in the South Carolina Department of Archives and History, Columbia.

The account of Swails's billiards game in Charleston is from the *Charleston Mercury*, March 18, 1868.

CHAPTER NINE

A Campaign of Intimidation and Terror

For typical descriptions of bribery schemes in which Swails was allegedly involved, see *Yorkville (SC) Inquirer*, May 3, 1877; *Pickens (SC) Sentinel*, March 28, 1878; and *Charleston Daily News*, August 26, 1870.

Details of events during Wade Hampton's political ascendency and the end of Reconstruction in South Carolina are in the works cited for chapters 7 and 8 as well as in Walter Brian Cisco, *Wade Hampton: Confederate Warrior, Conservative Statesman* (Washington, DC: Brassey's, 2004); Rod Andrew Jr., *Wade Hampton: Confederate Warrior to Southern Redeemer* (Chapel Hill: University of South Carolina Press, 2008); and Henry T. Thompson, *Ousting the Carpetbagger from South Carolina* (New York: R. L. Bryan, 1926). Descriptions of political events are also drawn from contemporaneous newspaper coverage. Trial Justice Black's letter to Governor Chamberlain dated October 2, 1876, is in the Chamberlain Papers, South Carolina Department of Archives and History, Columbia. The White Oak incident is described in Swails to Hampton, October 7, 1878, and Montgomery to President Grant, October 17, 1878, Swails Personal Papers.

CHAPTER TEN

What a Mockery of Justice Is This?

Hampton to Swails, October 24, 1878, Swails Personal Papers, was also printed in the *New York Times,* October 31, 1878. Swails's communications with Sheriff Jacobs are in Swails Personal Papers, while his political rivalry with Robert Smalls is described in Edward A. Miller Jr., *Gullah Statesman: Robert Smalls, from Slavery to Congress, 1839–1915* (Columbia: University of South Carolina Press, 1995).

CHAPTER ELEVEN

A Proper Denouement to an Extraordinary Man

Swails's representation of Smalls is from House Committee on Elections, *Robert Smalls v. William Elliott,* H. Rpt. 3536, 50th Cong., 2nd sess., December 7, 1888; Miller, *Gullah Statesman,* 166–70; and *Congressional Record,* 50th Cong., 2nd sess., 1808–13, App. 74. Some of his correspondence with Smalls and with former members of the 54th Massachusetts are in Swails Personal Papers.

Swails's last days are reconstructed from documents including, among others, Sanitarium Receipt, March 9, 1899 (a three-week stay, including room, board, nursing, medical care, and ordinary medicines); Chairman of Kingstree, SC, Board of Health, Autopsy Report, May 17, 1900; Henry A. Cauth to F. Grant Swails, March 10, 1899; George A. Cooper to Swails, April 1, 1899; and George W. Jackson to Swails, April 1, 1899, Swails Personal Papers. Additional information is collected in MacDougall, "Search for Stephen Swails" (unpublished). Swails obituary, *Kingstree (SC) County Record,* May 24, 1900, front page.

Works cited in tracing Swails's reputation after his death include Samuel D. McGill, *Narrative of Reminiscences in Williamsburg County* (Columbia, SC: Bryan, 1897); Bodie, *History of Williamsburg County;* Henry E. Davis, "Address," in *Williamsburg Presbyterian Church, 1736–1881,* by Robert Witherspoon et al. (Kingstree, SC: Williamsburg Presbyterian Church, 1981); and Egerton, *Thunder at the Gates.*

INDEX